THE **POWER** OF **IDEAS**

FIVE PEOPLE WHO CHANGED THE URBAN LANDSCAPE

TERRY J. LASSAR | DOUGLAS R. PORTER

ULI–the Urban Land Institute
1025 Thomas Jefferson Street, N.W.
Suite 500 West
Washington, D.C. 20007-5201

Lassar, Terry J., and Douglas R. Porter.
  *The Power of Ideas: Five People Who Changed
  the Urban Landscape*
Washington, D.C.: ULI–the Urban Land Institute, 2004.

ISBN: 0-87420-930-7
Library of Congress Control Number: 2004110834

Printed in the United States of America.
10 9 8 7 6 5 4 3 2 1

CONTENTS

ABOUT THE AUTHORS

DOUGLAS R. PORTER is one of the nation's leading authorities on growth management at the state, regional, and local levels. He formed the nonprofit Growth Management Institute in 1992 to conduct research and education in growth management policies and practices. His work spans the spectrum from affordable housing to transportation/land use relationships and regional and community development issues. Porter has a master's degree in urban and regional planning from the University of Illinois.

TERRY J. LASSAR is a writer and a consultant. She covers real estate and land use issues nationwide and has published many articles and books on urban development, planning, architecture, and design; as well as on land use topics. She has a master's degree in English from the University of Virginia, and a J.D. from Washington University.

ACKNOWLEDGMENTS

WE ARE INDEBTED to a host of people for their help and support in preparing this book. First, thanks to the Nichols family, in particular Wayne Nichols and Jeannette Nichols, for establishing the ULI J.C. Nichols Prize for Visionaries in Urban Development. Thanks to all the individuals who shared their insights about and experiences with the five prizewinners—they are listed at the end of each chapter. We are also indebted to many people at the Urban Land Institute: Ann Oliveri and Rachelle Levitt for their inspiration; Gayle Berens for her unflagging support and thoughtful work with the manuscript; David Takesuye for his research assistance; Rick Davis, ULI's information specialist, who culled out numerous books and articles for us; Nancy Stewart and Micaela Porta (of Engine Books) for their sensitive editing; and Betsy VanBuskirk for her fine design work.

TERRY J. LASSAR
DOUGLAS R. PORTER

FOREWORD

AMERICAN CULTURE HAS ALWAYS HAD a delicate, not to say adversarial, relationship with the urban impulse. We may have a lot of cities in this country, but we don't always like them, or believe them to be central to our identity as a civilization. Thomas Jefferson, of course, hoped we could all but do without cities, and if his 18th-century vision of the United States as a rural and agrarian society came to seem impractical after the Industrial Revolution, it is hard not to believe that a vast number of Americans still find it alluring.

Somehow, almost in spite of ourselves, we managed to make great cities in the early decades of the 20th century, a time when New York, Chicago, Boston, Pittsburgh, Philadelphia, Minneapolis, Buffalo, St. Louis, Cleveland, Detroit, and Kansas City—to name but a few—grew to possess a powerful and civilizing urbanism. Then, in the second half of the century, we proceeded to rip this magnificent creation apart, as the automobile allowed our anti-urban tendencies to flourish once more. Sometimes we sold our cities short in the guise of social responsibility, pretending that we were renewing them when we were actually destroying them with expressways and sterile towers; at other times, we masked our anti-urban sentiments in the genteel middle-class garb of suburbanization.

If we have never truly been the rural country of Jefferson's dreams, neither are we the urban culture that Alexander Hamilton envisioned. Most Americans in truth favor the world in between—the benign suburban landscape in which private space is elevated above that of public space, and there is at least the illusion of safety, comfort, and plenty for all.

The ULI J.C. Nichols Prize for Visionaries in Urban Development was created to honor one of the great real estate developers of modern times, a man who knew that the act of building is also the act of creating community, and who saw his mission as trying to tie the quest for comfort and beauty with the larger calling of community. J.C. Nichols understood that successful real estate developments do not exist in a vacuum—that they need to make economic sense, they need to make aesthetic sense, and most of all they need to make social sense—and the projects that do best are the ones that enrich their surroundings.

What joins together all five of the initial winners of the Nichols Prize—Joseph Riley, Daniel Patrick Moynihan, Gerald Hines, Vincent Scully, and Richard Baron—is that they all share Nichols's sense of the city as a public realm, as the physical embodiment of the idea of common ground. They have always been aware that great cities do not come accidentally, and that ennobling urban places are not built easily. There is a paradox involved in the making of cities that all of the Nichols Prize winners have, I believe, understood: they know that for all that cities may go against the American grain, they represent our highest ideals.

It is right that in its first five years, the prize has gone to a public official who changed the face of one of our most beloved cities; to a scholar-politician who was a passionate and articulate advocate of greater public architecture; to a developer who showed that design could have a profound impact on the marketplace and who, like J.C. Nichols himself, has taken on the building of projects that sought to establish a broader urban context; to one of America's greatest architectural historians who has influenced generations of students through his powerful arguments for the meaning of community and the connection between architecture and the quality of life; and to a developer who has consistently believed in development with a social conscience, and has proven that social responsibility and business success are not incompatible.

The accomplishments of each of these winners are extraordinary; the range they represent is even more so. Together, they embrace all of the qualities that the ULI J.C. Nichols Prize—and, indeed, the Urban Land Institute itself—was created to support. For all that the five winners are different from each other, they have one important thing in common. Each in his own way reminds us that ideas and action are inseparable in the making of cities. Every one of the Nichols Prize winners is a citizen whose mission is to use ideas to improve the quality of life, and they are all driven by a deep and passionate belief not only in the value of cities, but in their urgency. They believe, too, in the new, and in the need to see our cities not only as a great gift from the past that is our obligation to preserve and protect, but also as a laboratory for the future. Each of them, in his own way, sees the city as a place of promise.

Paul Goldberger
Dean, Parsons School of Design
Architecture Critic, *New Yorker*

INTRODUCTION

THIS BOOK CELEBRATES THE FIVE-YEAR ANNIVERSARY of the Urban Land Institute's distinguished award program—the ULI J.C. Nichols Prize for Visionaries in Urban Development—and profiles the five extraordinary recipients from 2000 through 2004.

The J.C. Nichols Prize furthers ULI's mission: to provide responsible leadership in the use of land to enhance the total environment. The annual prize was established in January 2000 to recognize individuals and representatives from institutions who provide unique leadership by inspiring enlightened urban development that enhances the overall quality of life in America's communities. How we build, how we shape our environment have a profound and lasting impact on how we live. In this way, the Nichols Prize is a visible symbol of the critical role that development plays in building community, strengthening our cities, and enriching our lives.

The $100,000 prize honors the legacy of legendary developer Jesse Clyde Nichols (1880–1950), of Kansas City, Missouri. The prize is funded by an endowment by the Nichols family. A founding member of ULI, J.C. Nichols is widely regarded as one of America's most influential entrepreneurs in urban development during the first half of the 20th century. Part of his enduring legacy are the Country Club Plaza, one of the country's oldest shopping centers; the Country Club district, a model residential neighborhood; and numerous other well-preserved residential neighborhoods in Kansas City.

Wayne Nichols, the grandson of J.C. Nichols, says his grandfather understood the difference between building mere subdivisions linked by streets and utility lines, and building whole neighborhoods in which people feel connected and a sense of community. In the early 1900s, Nichols and some of his peers took train trips to visit each other's developments. They would throw their plans out on the

ULI J.C. NICHOLS PRIZE WINNERS

2000
JOSEPH P. RILEY, JR.
MAYOR OF
CHARLESTON,
SOUTH CAROLINA

2001
DANIEL PATRICK MOYNIHAN
FORMER U.S. SENATOR

2002
GERALD D. HINES
FOUNDER AND
CHAIRMAN
HINES

2003
VINCENT SCULLY
ARCHITECTURAL
HISTORIAN

2004
RICHARD D. BARON
CHAIRMAN
McCORMACK BARON
SALAZAR

1

table, critique them, and work together to flesh out a viable design. "Their goal," according to Wayne Nichols, "was to create beautiful communities—not subdivisions, not shopping centers—but long-term, integrated planned communities. They saw themselves as building human environments. Their motto was 'land development is a responsibility, not a right.'"

The presentation of the first ULI J.C. Nichols Prize for Visionaries in Urban Development in 2000 coincided with the 50th anniversary of the J.C. Nichols Foundation (now the ULI Foundation), created in 1950 by ULI trustees to perpetuate Nichols's ideals. In the 1940s, Nichols worked to create the Institute's Community Builders Council (CBC) to provide a forum for industry professionals in the United States and Canada to exchange ideas and offer analyses of real estate practices. CBC meetings led to the publication of the *Community Builders Handbook,* produced by Nichols, which was the first authoritative publication on community planning and the forerunner to subsequent ULI development handbooks. The objectives of the CBC are carried out today by a wide range of specialized ULI councils.

The individuals selected to serve on the prize award juries represent some of the most esteemed names in the urban development field. They also represent the diversity of professionals who ultimately shape our built environment and influence the quality of life in our cities—designers, financiers, developers, educators, and journalists.

The prize is awarded to a living person who meets the following criteria: who individually, or as a representative of his or her organization, has made a distinguished contribution to community building in North America; whose visionary standards of excellence in the land use and development field have proven their permanence and worth; who is committed to a built environment of the highest quality; and whose example inspires the highest level of development practice.

Each of the recipients recognized that future generations will remember us for the buildings and urban places we leave behind. Each viewed the city as a common ground for all citizens to enjoy.

And each aspired to create memorable urban places. Each of the five J.C. Nichols prizewinners also used his exceptional leadership capacities to successfully carry out his vision.

The two political leaders in the group applied their enormous powers of persuasion and influence to make government a force behind good architecture and urban design. Both men understood that city building and rebuilding take a long time. They never set aside their long-range views of urban issues in favor of quick-fix pursuits to parade before voters in their next election. Daniel Patrick Moynihan spent half a lifetime revitalizing Pennsylvania Avenue and Joseph Riley has dedicated much of his career to renewing downtown Charleston.

The two developers in the group were propelled by a similar determination and insuperable energy to take on incredibly ambitious and challenging projects that would improve our cities. Richard Baron recognized the disastrous consequences of separating low-income families from the rest of the community. Economically integrated housing was the starting point of his lifelong work to rebuild lost neighborhoods in cities around the country. Gerald Hines, who became known as a patron of finely crafted buildings—a "modern Medici"—has proved that design can have a powerful influence on the marketplace. Driven to excel, Hines raised the bar for commercial development worldwide and aspired to build a larger urban context.

THE URBAN LAND INSTITUTE
J.C. NICHOLS PRIZE
FOR VISIONARIES IN
URBAN DEVELOPMENT

The scholar and teacher in the group, Vincent Scully, has been uniquely persuasive in conveying his particular grasp of socially conscious architecture, what he calls "the architecture of community." He incisively transformed the ways that generations of architects and urban designers think about buildings and their settings and, through their work, the form and quality of our urban communities.

Like J.C. Nichols, these five visionaries used the power of ideas to change the urban landscape. They applied their passion, intellect, and bold leadership to realize their dreams. And in the process, they changed the way we think about and build our cities.

A CITY SHOULD BE A PLACE WITH SUCH BEAUTY
AND ORDER THAT IT IS INSPIRATIONAL.

JOSEPH P. RILEY, JR.

JOSEPH P. RILEY, JR.

CARING FOR CITIES

JOSEPH P. RILEY, JR., has devoted his life to caring for cities. The city he has cared for the longest is Charleston, South Carolina, where he was elected mayor in 1975 and has served ever since. He has no formal training in architecture or urban design, but he is known as the master designer of his city and has won many of the most prestigious design awards in the country. Mayor Riley learned by walking, observing, and reading. He also learned from the many talented designers he has worked with over the years. But the best teacher, according to Riley, is the city.

Riley believes that cities are "the lasting mark of a civilization." And although Americans, until recently, have been fleeing them by the millions, he says we need our cities more than ever. What goes on in the center is what "sparks and shapes life for the entire region around it," he notes. "Cities give us memories. Every time we can keep a piece of historic texture and scale, we are giving something to future generations that they will revere, a sense of place."[i]

GREAT CITIES HAVE THE GUTS TO GIVE THE FINEST PARTS OF THEIR CITY TO THE PUBLIC REALM. JOSEPH P. RILEY, JR.

Many people have seen the mayor's legendary slide show that tells the story of the revival of Charleston's central city. One of the last images shows a workman holding a blowtorch as he bevels the edges of a large bluestone paver that will form part of a sidewalk in the city's downtown. The workman is kneeling on his hands and knees, attending to a fine detail. "This," says Riley, "is the way we must care for our cities, like treasures."

MAKING THE TABLE BIGGER

Civil rights, to a great extent, got Joe Riley started in politics. Soon after graduating from the University of South Carolina School of Law, he was elected to the South Carolina House of

Representatives in 1968, where he served for six years. A member of the "Young Turks," a group of young legislators of the progressive wing of the Democratic party, Riley had developed a reputation as a reformer, especially on civil rights and social justice issues.

In 1975, Charleston's black leaders and the city's mainly white business community asked the 32-year-old Riley to run for mayor. The city was experiencing severe racial tensions. Civic leaders wanted to avoid the strife of the previous mayoral race that had divided the city along racial lines. Based on his progressive track record in the legislature, Joe Riley, it was felt, could bridge the divide. "Had it not been for that need," says Riley, "I would never have run for mayor."

Joseph P. Riley, Jr., mayor of Charleston, 1975 to the present.

BILL MURTON, CITY OF CHARLESTON

Joe Riley offered a new image of moving the city forward. He ran on a platform of downtown revitalization, reducing crime, increasing low-income housing, and improving public transit. This Charleston native, who had grown up in the staid "South of Broad" neighborhood—the wealthiest section of town—would bring about three decades of sweeping reforms that would forever change his city.

First, he worked to heal racial tensions. The number of blacks on the city council was increased by 50 percent. He opened the government to African Americans, to give them "complete citizenship," he said. African Americans, who currently make up 34 percent of Charleston's population of some 100,000, hold major posts in the city. But Riley is quick to point out, "We didn't run anyone away from the table; we just made the table bigger."

"One of the nicest compliments I've ever received," relates Riley, was from an African American man who came to him six months after he took office. "He said, 'Joe, I think you're moving too fast, doing too much in the black community and it's hurting you politically.' Behind my back, some people called me LBJ, for Little Black Joe. But you don't hear that anymore."

Riley knew it was important to break down the deep distrust of the police department in the black community. When his police chief died, he appointed Reuben Greenberg in 1982, the city's first black police chief. Greenberg, a pioneer in community-oriented policing, took officers out of their cars and sent them out into the neighborhoods on foot and bicycle. Crime declined sharply. Charleston's police department is regarded as one of the country's best trained and most successful. Mirroring the mayor's own hands-on leadership style, Greenberg is known to set out on rollerblades, or be found on a street corner directing traffic. The multitalented Greenberg, in addition to his training in law enforcement and administration, also earned a master's degree in city planning. His book, *Let's Take Back Our Streets*, was published in 1989.

BEAUTIFUL PUBLIC HOUSING

When Riley was elected mayor, many sections of Charleston were in a sorry state of decay. The city was pockmarked with abandoned buildings and vacant lots. He first concentrated redevelopment efforts in the poorest parts of the city, mostly in African American neighborhoods. Like most other cities, Charleston had its share of public housing projects built during the 1940s and 1950s. Soon after Riley took office, the city's housing authority was about to build another low-income housing tower. But the young mayor said no. "That would ignore the collective experience of Western civilization about building human-scale neighborhoods, with thousands of strings of affection and respect to tie together residents of all income levels," he said. Instead of segregating public housing, Riley wanted the subsidized homes to be scattered throughout the city.

Before most cities were experimenting with new designs for low-income housing and long before the start of the federal government's HOPE VI program for mixing market-rate and subsidized housing, Charleston was building low-income housing that blended with the neighborhoods. "Every building constructed, every house rehabilitated—no matter how modest, is expected to be beautiful," asserts Riley. When an architect came in with ugly, barren designs for low-income houses, he remembers, "We sent him back to the drawing board. And when he persisted in designing institutional-style houses, we fired him."

WE MUST FEEL THAT WE ARE HOLDING THEM [CITIES] TEMPORARILY IN OUR HANDS, AS WE WOULD A FINE FAMILY HEIRLOOM. AND WE ARE TO PASS THEM ON TO FUTURE GENERATIONS IN JUST AS BEAUTIFUL CONDITION—IF NOT MORE BEAUTIFUL—AS THE WAY WE FOUND THEM.
JOSEPH P. RILEY, JR.

Prince Charles visited Charleston in 1990 and specifically asked to see one of the newly created scattered-site public housing units. As a student of architecture, he felt that Charleston had an important lesson to teach about building better, beautiful housing for poor people. He visited the home of an elderly lady. "She was amazingly at ease when she met with him," recalls Riley. "She knew he was to be the next king of England, but she also knew that she lived in a handsome home—an apartment with a street number, not a unit in some monolith. She felt a sense of ownership and that made her proud."

Some of the city's scattered-site homes have spurred private redevelopment around them. President Reagan, in a ceremony at the White House in 1985, presented Mayor Riley with a Presidential Award for Design Excellence for public housing in Charleston. The city's designs for low-income housing have won other national design awards, including several from the American Institute of Architects.

POSITIVE STEPS

Mayor Riley says he never expected to be mayor for 29 years. In 1994, he ran for governor but lost the runoff for the Democratic party nomination by a slim margin. Four years later, he was asked to run again, but declined. In 2000, he entered the national political arena with his "Get in Step" march to remove the Confederate flag from atop the South Carolina State House.

"One day the mayor walked into the office, "says David Agnew, who was Mayor Riley's executive assistant for five years. "He said, 'Maybe I've had too much coffee this morning, but I want to walk to the state capital and send a message to everyone in the state that there are South Carolinians who want the flag to come down.'" For too long this incendiary symbol had sowed deep divisions among people of the state.

BILL MURTON, CITY OF CHARLESTON

Riley organized the four-day march to Columbia, South Carolina. The 116-mile walk was a plea to the legislature to "get in step with the people of South Carolina." Riley invited a number of influential South Carolinians to join the march, including Hugh McColl, Jr., chief executive of Bank of America, and Darla Moore, an investor who had recently made a $25 million gift to the University of South Carolina. Press coverage was extensive, and the world took note. The march sent a clear message that citizens from all walks of life in South Carolina supported this protest. Mayor Riley knew he would be ridiculed and physically threatened, both of which occurred, says Agnew. But the rewards of bold action outweighed the risks. The flag came down, eventually.

Riley leads "Get in Step" march to remove Confederate flag from the South Carolina State House.

REVISITING CHARLESTON'S PAINFUL PAST

Riley says that one of the achievements of which he is especially proud is the racial harmony that now prevails in his city. Racial inequality had always been deeply rooted in Charleston's past. For more than a century, the city was the principal port of entry for African slaves into British North America. But the sorrowful, painful subject of slavery had never been memorialized.

It was Riley's idea to build an International African American History Museum in Charleston. The first major institution of this kind, the museum will trace the slave trade history from Africa to America. Mayor Riley told *New York Times* reporter Stephen Kinzer, "The whole country has matured in terms of our willingness to confront slavery. We as a culture need to do this as part of our progress in coming together and healing."[ii] Riley envisions a national museum that will interest African Americans and everyone else, much the same way that the Holocaust Museum in Washington and museums about Native Americans interest all people.

Former president Bill Clinton accepted Riley's invitation to serve as honorary chairman of the museum's International Committee. James E. Clyburn, the first African American to represent South Carolina in the Congress since Reconstruction, chairs the Working Committee and provides active leadership for the museum. Plans are underway for raising some $60 million for the new building.

BILL MURTON, CITY OF CHARLESTON

REVIVING THE CENTER

Mayor Riley has lived almost his entire life in Charleston, where he was born 61 years ago. This extraordinarily beautiful coastal city, founded in 1670, was left worn and poverty-stricken by the Civil War. Charleston's economic misfortune ultimately helped preserve its renowned architecture. Without the means to reconstruct and modernize, Charleston found itself in the early 20th century with a unique collection of buildings spanning 200 years of architectural styles, from Georgian to federal and Victorian. But the 1920s brought prosperity to Charleston and, with it, demolition. Concerned citizens founded a powerful preservation advocacy group, and soon afterward, Charleston passed the country's first zoning ordinance to protect historic structures. The city's reputation as a preservation pioneer continues today.

Charleston Place, the catalyst for the city's revival, features street-facing shops.

When Riley took office, the Charleston peninsula was losing population at the rate of nearly 13 percent a year. Some 27 percent of its 70,000 citizens lived below the poverty level. Once known as the "Convention City of the South," Charleston had lost seven hotels in the previous two decades. With more than 1 million square feet of vacant commercial space on the city's main street, the central business core was ailing.

The new mayor worked closely with area businesspeople on a strategy for resuscitating the central business district. They decided on a plan to build a large luxury hotel with meeting rooms, retail shops, and a public parking garage in the heart of the business district. The development would fill a derelict block on King Street, the city's main retail artery, and would connect with another major shopping street to be a catalyst for reviving the downtown.

Mayor Riley had no inkling then that this project would be the toughest one of his career. Back then, he recalls, cities were in bad shape. Charleston was hurting. Downtown was dying. Riley viewed this project as a catalyst for growth and a way to revive the central business district for both residents and tourists. He never dreamed that the project would spark fierce opposition.

The opposition was led by one of the city's two powerful preservation groups, which worried that this "convention center" (as they called it) would overwhelm the historic downtown. They looked to New Orleans's commercialized French Quarter as an example of what they wanted to avoid. They also objected to the demolition of more than a dozen older buildings. They brought a series of legal actions that delayed Charleston Place, which took nine years to complete.

Meanwhile, the original developer ran into financial problems and eventually backed out of the deal. Riley brought in new development partners, who were much better attuned to the desires of the community, including the preservationists. Baltimore-based Cordish Embry & Associates teamed up with the seasoned shopping mall magnate A. Alfred Taubman to redesign the center. They removed four stories from the central hotel building, brought many of the retail shops out onto the street, and kept more of the older buildings. Riley recalls that the buildings on the site were in dismal shape: "A couple of strip joints, old turn-of-the century mercantile storefronts with ugly brick infill. But we knew that demolishing them would remove forever the memories of those buildings." So the city worked with the owners to renovate the old buildings, cut off the backs, and place parking behind.

"We knew we were putting Charleston Place in a sick part of town," says Riley, "but we also knew that if we got the right critical mass there, the area would come back to life." And it did. Now, even during the dog days of summer when the city's steamy weather might dampen tourist interest, Charleston Place, which opened in 1986, is booked solid. The $100 million development drew luxury local shops and branches of high-end national stores. The street-facing shops and eateries, thronged with visitors and residents, are busy year-round.

The immensely complicated financing arrangement for Charleston Place demonstrates the mayor's sixth sense for deal making. Charleston developer John Darby notes, "[Riley] is a master at mobilizing public/private partnerships. . . . [he] knew how to get the biggest bang for the buck with federal grants, and knew how to leverage them to the fullest extent." Riley secured more than $18 million from the federal government, in addition to the funds he raised from city bonds and state highway funds.

GIFT TO THE FUTURE

The second toughest project of Riley's career was Waterfront Park. In the late 1970s, a developer approached the city with plans to build several mixed-use towers on a weedy shore where the Cooper River flows into Charleston Harbor. Many people said the proposal made good business sense. It would have cleaned up a blighted section of town and instantly added prime real estate to the tax rolls. But Riley said no. This land, he claimed, belonged to all of Charleston and shouldn't be limited to the enjoyment of only the wealthy. Riley envisioned a beautiful linear park, where all Charlestonians, as well as the city's many visitors, would be welcome to stroll along the riverside and enjoy the fresh breezes.

But Riley's idea was controversial. Parks cost a lot of money. They are difficult and expensive to maintain. People loiter in them. Undeterred, the mayor worked to sell his vision to the public and gain support from the city council. He arranged for a land swap, and secured the financing to purchase and develop the 13-acre site for Waterfront Park, which he called "a gift to the future."

Stuart Dawson, with the nationally known landscape architecture firm Sasaki, local landscape architect Ed Pinckney, and New York architect and urban designer Jaquelin Robertson, whose firm Cooper, Robertson & Partners had designed the famously successful Battery Park along the Hudson River at the base of Wall Street, were hired to design Waterfront Park. Built with a combination of public and private funds, it offers a series of quiet living room–like sitting areas—a grassy public green, a fountain for children to cool off in the summer, benches, and a magnificent pier.

The park's several garden "rooms," which are separated by small hedges, have benches for meditation, reading, or simply relaxing. It was Riley's idea to install adult-size bench swings in covered pavilions on the park's pier. He rejected a proposal to ban children from splashing in the park's Vendue Fountain and insisted that all areas remain open to the public.

Riley claims that it is just as important to design the use of a park as the physical plan. Other parks in the city have sports fields and venues for

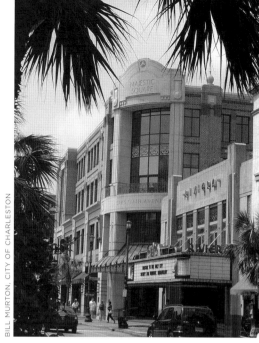
BILL MURTON, CITY OF CHARLESTON

Riley mobilized the public/private partnership to develop Majestic Square.

BILL MURTON, CITY OF CHARLESTON

The famous pineapple fountain—an immediate icon for the city.

BILL MURTON, CITY OF CHARLESTON

Open for splashing: Waterfront Park's frolic-friendly fountains.

Bench swings for adults on the Waterfront Park's pier.

Charleston city art gallery.

concerts. But Waterfront Park was planned as a place of peace and repose. A sign prominently displayed at the park forbids radios, mopeds, and skateboards.

Riley knew that Waterfront Park would boost significantly the value of adjacent land parcels. Therefore, when the city eventually sold one of these parcels in the late 1990s to a developer for luxury housing, it required specific public amenities that would benefit all Charleston residents. The development deal was structured so that after a certain return from development, the city shared in the profits, which were used to build affordable housing elsewhere in Charleston. View corridors and public rights-of-way were strictly maintained so that pedestrians can walk easily through the development to Waterfront Park. The public/private agreement also required developer Vendue Associates to build a handsome city art gallery, which was financed by the $3 million penthouse built above it. The luxury condominiums fit the low-rise scale of the city's historic French Quarter.

MANAGING OUR CITIES

An important part of caring for cities is managing how they are used. Early on, Riley and his advisers decided to expand the city's tourist business into a year-round industry. Charleston's distinctive, historic architecture has always been a main attraction. People come to see the colonial and antebellum mansions, the fountains, cobblestone streets, and wrought-iron balconies and gates. But tourism, which had long been a mainstay of the city's economy, flagged during the 1950s and 1960s. Fifty years ago, Charleston was a seasonal tourist destination. Visitors came mainly in April and May to see the gardens and restored houses. Today, more than 4.6 million people visit the city during the course of the year. For 17 days in late spring, Charleston becomes the nation's cultural capital when the Spoleto Festival USA and the companion local Piccolo Arts Festival turn the city into one huge stage for world-class music, dance, and theater events.

Although tourism is serious business in Charleston, Riley emphasizes that the city's residents have always been the first priority. "You don't make a city beautiful just to attract visitors. If you make a city special for those who live there, then the tourists will come," says the mayor. Moreover, he believes city officials "have a management responsibility to organize the way people use their city." And manage it, he has.

Riley set up a tourism management program in the mid-1980s to control the more burdensome consequences of tourism that plague many other cities. Crowds, buses, and carriages, especially in the historic neighborhoods, are carefully monitored. The city's tourism management ordinance limits the number of tour buses permitted at any one time in designated areas downtown. Charleston was one of the first cities to require diapers for horses that pull carriages in the downtown. "One horse and buggy, no problem," says Riley, "but when you have 30 carriages, that's a problem." Tour guides and tour vehicles—buses and horse-drawn carriages—must be certified. Tour vehicles may not exceed certain dimensions, and all logos and colors must be approved by the tourism commission. All carriages must depart from the City Market area and are permitted to travel only within three zones. A gatekeeper system was devised to control the number of carriages in a zone at any one time.

BILL MURTON, CITY OF CHARLESTON

The city controls the number of horse-drawn carriages to protect nearby residential neighborhoods.

Charleston's historic district, which is primarily residential, is the city's "golden egg." Vanessa Turner-Maybank, who has led the city's tourism management program since the start, says the program aims to protect the quality of life of the residents while accommodating the city's robust tourist industry. "It's a delicate balance," she notes. Charleston has been a leader in this field. Turner-Maybank and her staff have advised other cities including Savannah, New Orleans, and San Antonio, which have patterned their tourism management programs after Charleston's.

Visitors are encouraged to walk the city, but walking tours are also regulated; no more than 20 pedestrians with one guide at a time. The city built a stunning visitors center in a remodeled 19th-century railroad warehouse. The center was strategically located on the edge of downtown with a large public garage next door so that people would park and leave their cars. At the visitors center, people can pick up maps, view orientation films, and then board shuttle buses to get around town.

Charleston also controls the location of new hotels. Although the city encourages new hotel development, it wants them to locate where they strengthen the public realm—on main streets to get people out walking and generate activity—which "may not be where they make the most money," adds Riley. So hotels are steered to specific locations and barred from others like the waterfront, which is to be kept open for the public. As tourism flourished during the last decade, new hotels saturated the city's oldest historic district. The city responded with additional controls that steered large new hotels to other neighborhoods where the city is encouraging growth. Channeling hotels to preferred locations is part of the city's tourism management approach. "It's all about getting visitors to the parts of the city where you want them," Riley explains.

In addition to managing visitors' use of the city, Charleston uses other creative controls to enforce its reasonable code of gentility. One example is the list of rules for using Waterfront Park and other city parks. Another is the 6:00 p.m. deadline for carriage drivers to leave residential neighborhoods. The noise ordinance, aimed at late-night activity in restaurants and bars, also applies to vehicles that play music too boisterously in residential neighborhoods. Two years ago, Mayor Riley set up a special "Livability Court" to address these types of disturbances, as well as cases involving animal nuisance and unkempt property. The rationale was that in municipal court, such cases frequently take a back seat to criminal cases. The Livability Court, which won the U.S. Conference of Mayors' 2004 City Livability Award, was established to direct full attention to quality-of-life issues.

MASTER DESIGNER

Riley doesn't apologize for micromanaging his city, especially when it concerns physical design. He believes that public officials, especially mayors, have a responsibility to influence the way their cities look. Whether it's the design of a utilitarian pump station or a parking garage, every design detail matters.

The mayor delights in telling the story of selecting gravel for a path in Waterfront Park. He wanted gravel that would crunch when people walked on it, to mute the hard sounds of the city. Color was just as important. The initial samples were all boring gray, he says. So he went on a search that lasted two years. Every new place the mayor went, he studied the gravel. This process also involved a few instances of surreptitiously pocketing samples from notable public gardens, including the

Victorian garden at the Smithsonian Institution in Washington. Riley concedes, "One woman on my parks staff finally quit out of frustration, said I'd gone wacko. But we eventually came up with the perfect gravel mix that crunches just right. It's like grandma's pound cake recipe with ten different ingredients," he says. Mayor Riley buoyantly points out that the reddish-brown gravel path between the lawn and the Cooper River is dense enough to accommodate wheelchairs, and the gravel's color is a pleasing transition from the park to the water.

The mayor devotes equal attention to the design of parking garages. Parking garages don't have to resemble aircraft carriers. In fact, they shouldn't look like garages at all. Riley brought New York architect and urban designer Jaquelin Robertson to work in Charleston in the late 1970s. Robertson helped the city craft design guidelines "to civilize" parking facilities. The guidelines call for shops and restaurants on the ground floor, and, whenever possible, parking structures are to be buried behind development, away from main shopping streets. The mayor has also devised different ways to transform small parking lots in the middle of the city into "urban rooms," using brick walls, greenery, and flowers. As a result, Charleston boasts some of the finest looking parking facilities in the country. According to Riley, cities too often make the mistake of looking to suburban models. Developers of suburban regional shopping malls feel compelled to build vast seas of parking as well as large parking garages that can be spotted easily from a highway nearby. This model, says Riley, is totally wrong for the city.

Riley also worked to implement a 50-foot-height cap in the downtown that had been recommended in a 1975 historic plan for the peninsula. Historic urban fabrics like that of Charleston are fragile; one of the biggest threats to historic downtowns is high-rise development, claims Robertson.

BILL MURTON, CITY OF CHARLESTON

Design guidelines for parking garages call for shops and restaurants on the ground floor.

In the beginning, some developers bristled at the barrage of new rules—"aesthetic regulations"— for building in the city, admits Riley. But they soon appreciated clear communication of the city's goals. By setting explicit ground rules about building heights, design of garages, and protection of vistas, the city works with developers to achieve their economic goals within these parameters.

Before attending law school, Joe Riley was an undergraduate at the Citadel in Charleston. He never formally studied design. Riley learned from able teachers like Jaquelin Robertson and notable landscape architects like Stuart Dawson and Laurie Olin. He recounts that when he first was elected mayor, he bought the *New York Times* every Sunday to read the articles on architecture and urban design by Paul Goldberger, who was then the *Times'* architecture critic. Riley also taught a course on planning and urban design at the College of Charleston more than 20 years ago.

BILL MURTON, CITY OF CHARLESTON

Early in his career, Mayor Riley participated in a Marshall Fellowship tour in England and Germany. A defining moment, he says, was a visit to a small town on the coast of England. He was impressed by the costly, beautiful materials that were used in public areas, such as the granite—instead of concrete—street curbs, and the large street trees and carefully manicured parks. These towns, recalls Riley, were not a bit timid about investing in their public realm. They recognized that investments in high-quality parks and beautiful streets were gifts to all citizens. "And that experience awakened me," says Riley. It was part of the inspiration for the Mayors' Institute on City Design that he helped found in 1986.

Even the drainage pump station on the edge of downtown is designed as an outstanding civic project.

That critical experience also motivated the mayor to create a beautiful public realm in Charleston, which he defines broadly: not only city-owned buildings and parks, but basically everything Charlestonians encounter when they step outside their homes—the city's streets and alleyways, as well as shops, restaurants, and theaters. Almost all the concrete curbs in downtown Charleston have been replaced with granite curbs. The city has repaired many of its bluestone sidewalks, which were first laid in the late 19th century, and also replaced many of the more recent concrete sidewalks with new bluestone pavers.

"There is no excuse," Riley says, "for anything to ever be built that does not add to the beauty of a city." Like the great city builders of earlier eras, he equates public design with civic responsibility. A good example is the huge drainage pump station on the edge of downtown that was made to look beautiful, the way the Romans built their public works, notes Riley. He views the space between buildings—sidewalks, streets, and green space—as the "democratic space of a city owned by its citizens, which must be beautifully designed to give people a sense of pride, affection, and connection with their city."

Because investment in the public realm is for the benefit of all citizens, such expenditures require no apology, according to Riley. He tells the story of building the city baseball stadium on a difficult, but beautiful waterfront parcel northwest of downtown. One of his rivals in a mayoral race claimed that Riley should have selected a different parcel on the edge of town—a piece of land that wouldn't have cost the city any money. Riley responded that when you build something for the public—a baseball stadium, an aquarium, or a waterfront park—you don't look for free land; you want the best land.

AMERICAN CULTURE HAS NOT BEEN ONE IN WHICH A PASSION FOR BEAUTY AND HIGH-QUALITY DESIGN IN CITIES HAS BEEN REVERED. SINCE WE ARE THE MOST URBAN NATION IN THE WORLD, THIS IS A PASSION THAT OUR CULTURE MUST EMBRACE, AND QUICKLY.
JOSEPH P. RILEY, JR.

When people talk to the mayor about their baseball stadium, they don't usually discuss the games, says Riley. They're more impressed by the spectacular setting. "People come up to me, they tell me about the sunsets," he says, "about looking out onto the water, which looks like an observation deck at a national park. It's all about enhancing the public realm," he notes.

URBAN DESIGN 101 FOR MAYORS

Just as Mayor Riley recognized the important role he played as Charleston's master designer, so did he believe that other mayors also could influence the direction and quality of physical design in their cities. "When mayors leave office," Riley notes, "they are remembered for the development that was built when they served." But he knew that design and beauty were not the stuff of mayoral speeches.

Although mayors have a great influence over development in their communities, they rarely have training in urban design. Most mayors neither know how to talk to designers and developers, nor how to read the blueprints that come across their desks. "We [mayors] needed a place to become familiar with how urban design works," says Riley. Riley looked for a way to share his knowledge of designing cities with mayors across the country.

The opportunity came when his friend Jaquelin Robertson invited him to participate in a symposium, "The Politics of Design," which Robertson organized in 1984. The point of the symposium, says Robertson, was that "mayors for better or worse could profoundly affect the design in their cities." Robertson, who had worked for New York's Mayor Lindsay for more than six years, was convinced that city design policies were most effective when guided at the mayoral level. Two mayors—John Lindsay of New York, and Joseph Riley—were invited to share their experiences, along with a leading development director, Edward Logue, who headed development corporations for New Haven, Boston, and New York State, and noted urban sociologist Nathan Glazer.

The symposium was a huge success. Mayor Riley felt strongly that this kind of dialogue should continue as an ongoing institution and wrote up a plan to do so. Riley always said that as mayor, he was Charleston's chief design steward. And most other mayors had the same opportunity to shape the physical environment in their cities. As he wrote in a letter to Robertson several months after the 1984 symposium, "The more sensitive mayors are to good urban design issues of livability, scale, diversity, etc., the more able they will be to help develop higher quality. [Therefore] if we could institute a program aimed at increasing mayors' sophistication and interest in urban design, we could have a substantial impact on the quality of development in American cities."[iii]

Riley's dream was realized in 1986 when the Mayors' Institute on City Design held its first meeting at the University of Virginia in Charlottesville. Designed by Thomas Jefferson, who called it an "academic village," the university was an inspirational setting. "Joe had recently been elected president of the U.S. Conference of Mayors. So he brought in the mayors and I provided the background," recalls Robertson. Riley typically opened each session with his stirring presentation on rebuilding Charleston's downtown. Robertson involved Adele Chatfield-Taylor, who headed the National Endowment for the Arts Design Program, which agreed to fund the Mayors' Institute, as well as Joan Abrahamson, who was director of the Jefferson Institute in California.

The organizers devised a simple format that basically continues today. A small group of six to eight mayors from large and small cities in different regions of the country are invited, all expenses paid. Each mayor is required to present in person (without staff assistance) his or her city's most critical urban design problem. An interdisciplinary team of mostly design professionals, and sometimes other urban experts such as sociologists and finance experts, critique the problem, offering recommendations and solution strategies. Mayors are required to attend the program's full two-and-a-half days and are not permitted to bring any staff. No press or audience are allowed, eliminating any cause for grandstanding.

Architect and architecture writer Robert Campbell, who has participated in the institute since the beginning, notes that although mayors and designers use different vocabularies, they frequently are working toward the same purpose. Although the Mayors' Institute was set up to educate mayors about urban design, "as the designers learned to trust the mayors, they learned equally from them," Campbell observes. "One of the things that struck me," he continues, "is that the mayors and designers tended to agree on where their cities ought to be." But it was the Mayors' Institute that "gave them the confidence to trust their instincts," he says, instead of being swayed by the advice of traffic engineers, developers, advocacy groups, and other "experts." As confident clients, the mayors are better prepared to know what to demand from designers and developers.

One of the strengths of the program is its diverse representation. Mayors from mid-sized and smaller cities often learn that their urban design challenges are similar to those facing mayors of large metropolises. In the case of Cincinnati, the citizens had passed a tax levy to fund two new stadiums. The problem presented by then-Mayor Roxanne Qualls was where to put them. Both teams wanted the same riverfront site with dramatic views of the suspension bridge and easy parking. Meanwhile, a host of other major projects were also planned for the waterfront. Feedback from the Mayors' Institute session made Qualls realize that the city first needed an overall plan for the waterfront before making decisions on specific projects.

THE MAYORS' INSTITUTE, MORE THAN ANY OTHER THING THAT I'VE BEEN ACADEMICALLY AND PROFESSIONALLY INVOLVED WITH, HAS BEEN THE MOST EFFECTIVE VEHICLE FOR ADVANCING THE CAUSE OF CITY DESIGN IN TERMS OF PUBLIC POLICY. AND IT REMAINS THAT WAY. IT'S AN ENORMOUSLY POWERFUL INSTRUMENT.
JAQUELIN ROBERTSON, ARCHITECT AND URBAN DESIGNER

Former Milwaukee mayor, John Norquist, who now leads the Congress for the New Urbanism, has participated in several of the institute's sessions. One session corroborated his inclination to remove one of the city's freeways that severed downtown Milwaukee from the river. Contemplating a new Milwaukee convention center, he was also inspired by the design of Charleston Place, which tucks parking and large meeting spaces behind street-level shops instead of creating a vast dead spot in the middle of the downtown. "So many cities," observes Norquist, "spend millions of dollars on convention centers and stadiums and forget that it's the culture of the city, the urban lifestyle that draws visitors. People don't visit New York for the Javits Center; they go because they want to experience New York."

The institute met twice a year at the University of Virginia. To reach a wider audience, regional institutes were added in the 1990s and held at campuses around the country. The National Endowment for the Arts, which provides core funding for the Mayors' Institute, partners with the U.S. Conference of Mayors and the American Architectural Foundation, which administers the program. Well over 600 mayors have participated in the Mayors' Institute since it was founded in 1986. Two national institutes currently are held at the Riley Institute for Urban Affairs and Policy Studies at the College of Charleston, and four regional institutes are hosted at different academic institutions throughout the country.

At the same time that he was transforming Charleston into one of the most dynamic, appealing urban centers in the country, Mayor Riley was continuously involved in the Mayors' Institute.

Unlike most mayors, he has had the advantage of following through on many complicated city building programs over the long term. His city and his regime are inspirational models for mayors around the country.

In a 1995 progress report to the National Endowment for the Arts, Riley wrote, "Almost without exception, every mayor who attends the Mayors' Institute will tell you that those were the most valuable three days of their tenure as mayor. And almost without exception they will tell you that after the Mayors' Institute, they never look at their cities the same way again."

BOLD LEADERSHIP

Joe Riley views cities as ecosystems—living, growing organisms that require nourishment. He has spent his career building institutions that will nourish and sustain cities. In addition to the Mayors' Institute on City Design, he helped start the South Carolina Aquarium, Spoleto Festival USA, Charleston Maritime Center, City Art Gallery, Riley Institute for Urban Affairs and Policy Studies at the College of Charleston, and the future International Museum of African American History. These are only a few of the many institutions Mayor Riley spearheaded to enrich his city and to leave as legacies for future generations.

Ambitious projects like these take enormous patience and persistence. Charleston Place took nine years. Revitalization of Charleston's downtown was a quarter century in the making. Mayor Riley learned that reviving a moribund downtown is a marathon, not a sprint. City building is tough, says Riley, and it's not easy to sustain the high energy needed to keep projects like this moving. To surmount the difficult times, he says it's essential to have a course of action—a vision—which you "know in your heart is the right solution."

The galvanizing force behind such projects as Waterfront Park, Riley Baseball Stadium, the aquarium, and the city maritime center was Riley's bold vision of an urban waterfront with water's-edge access for all Charleston citizens and visitors to enjoy. He is immensely skilled in communicating his visions and inspiring others to join him in achieving them. He has a special capacity to persuade people and win the necessary political support. "One of our responsibilities as mayors," he says "is to be good salesmen." Joe Riley is a master salesman. He invites everyone to the table, listens to them, carefully weighs all the issues and competing arguments, then selects the most reasonable option that will best advance his vision, notes David Agnew, former executive assistant to the mayor. He once told a high school class that the true job of a leader is to understand the "best aspirations of citizens," then articulate these dreams in a way that gains their confidence and ultimately their support.

But he's also strong-minded, "and tenacious as hell," according to Lawrence O. Thompson, executive chief of staff to the mayor. "He just doesn't give up," says Thompson, but pursues his goals with unrelenting vigor, which is one of his great strengths.

Mayor Riley has a way with people. Gracious and engaging, he tells a good story and has a great wit. For example, in relating people's initial response to the city's scattered site program for low-income housing, he recalls, "It was kind of fun looking for sites to build public housing. You know, the average American doesn't wake up and turn to his spouse and say, 'Honey, wouldn't it be great to have public housing next door? We haven't had any of that before.'"

To many Charlestonians, Joe Riley is more a statesman than a politician. This eight-term mayor, who has an impressive track record, has earned the trust of his constituents. But even earlier in his career, people recognized that when Riley took a position on something, he had thoroughly studied the issues and mastered the details. His encyclopedic command of urban design and planning topics and close involvement with nearly every significant development project in the city, for example, attest to his hands-on leadership.

Although he is known for his unlimited patience and persistence, Mayor Riley takes bold, swift action when necessary. Such was the case with the Daniel Island annexation. Every jurisdiction in the area was eyeing the huge parcel of mostly forested land due north of downtown Charleston that the Guggenheim Foundation was finally ready to develop. The state was building a freeway there that would make the island accessible for the first time. Riley and his legal advisers devised a creative plan to annex much of the land. Quietly and quickly they orchestrated a surprise annexation in 1991 between Christmas and New Year. By bringing most of Daniel Island into Charleston, the city could influence the development there and discourage the owners from building a gated community. Daniel Island is being developed as a new urbanist community with stores and businesses serving nearby homes and with sidewalks and green strips connecting the entire project. "We wanted to focus on the qualities of new urbanism that we celebrate in downtown Charleston," notes Riley. Charleston has aggressively annexed other important outlying areas that have significantly added to the city's tax base.

Mayor Riley's strong leadership was nowhere more manifest than in his response to Hurricane Hugo. When Hurricane Hugo slammed into Charleston in 1989, he won universal praise for getting the city cleaned up and back on its feet. But it was the action he took before the storm hit that saved so many lives. Informed that Hugo would hit within two days, Riley asked his staff to call other cities that had experienced hurricanes in recent years. What had they learned? What would they do differently now? He learned that the damage from rising water is frequently more devastating than the swirling winds. With the benefit of hindsight, they said they would have evacuated much earlier than they did. With that information, Riley spent the next two days on the radio, on television, getting word out to the press—imploring the people of his city to leave before the storm hit. Hurricanes occur regularly in the Low Country. But Hugo, he said, was like none other they had experienced and would be far more devastating.

"He did a superb job convincing people to leave," recalls Barbara Vaughn, the city's director of public information. The mayor had been in office for more than a decade, and he had an impressive record, so people believed him. "I can't tell you," says Vaughn, "how many people came up to the mayor after Hugo and thanked him for convincing them to evacuate. Without his warning, they said they would never have left."

Soon after Hugo hit, the mayor held a press conference. He described the profound devastation. Many parts of the city had no water for many weeks. Some residents lost power for nearly a month. The entire electrical system between Charleston and Columbia had to be completely rebuilt. Help poured in from around the country.

At the same time, it was important to convey the message to the outside world that Charleston, although badly damaged, would survive and be ready to welcome tourists again. Hugo hit in September. The mayor was committed to cleaning up the city in time to host the January conference that Prince Charles had organized.

The city's historic fabric was severely damaged; Hugo tore off many a rooftop. Naturally, people wanted to immediately replace their roofs (many were slate). But the damage was so extensive that there was not a large enough supply of slate available to replace all the roofs. So there was considerable pressure to compromise and install asphalt shingles instead.

John Hildreth, southeastern director of the National Trust for Historic Preservation, credits Mayor Riley for upholding the city's high design standards and setting the tone for the quality of the repair. The mayor backed up the city's architectural review regulations that allow repairs, but according to standards set by the board of architectural review. Although people were allowed to put up temporary roofs, they were required to replace them later with better-quality, more historically appropriate materials. "This was a critical lesson for older communities around the country that undergo natural disasters," says Hildreth. "When you rebuild, it's important that it be sustainable and not alter the character of your community."

Riley feels deeply indebted to the many communities that sent rescue teams to Charleston when Hugo crippled the city. As is his way, he has returned the favor whenever possible. Charleston's team of disaster experts—police, fire fighters, and medical personnel—has given assistance to numerous cities on the East Coast that have been ravaged by hurricanes and tornadoes. David Agnew says that one of the motivations for building such an outstanding public safety department—Charleston has one of the highest-rated fire departments in the country—was to prepare the city to assist some of the communities that had helped it rebuild after Hugo.

In his first week on the job as executive assistant to the mayor, David Agnew recalls attending a meeting in McCormick County, South Carolina, where the mayor addressed a group of retired businessmen. Riley made his usual stirring presentation about using good design to turn around downtown Charleston. At the end of the talk, Agnew noticed that "everyone in the room—mostly retired Republicans from the Northeast—all had tears in their eyes." He knew at that moment that Joe Riley was an anomaly. Just a few days before, Agnew had observed the mayor embroiled in tough negotiations to win support for an increase to the city's sales tax. Agnew recognized that the mayor, who had just moved a group of conservative businessmen to tears with his inspirational vision of creating beautiful civic spaces, was equally comfortable working in this very different political realm of pragmatic deal making. And that's one of his great skills, his ability to straddle these two very different worlds.

Creating beautiful places for all citizens to own and enjoy is a moral imperative.

Charleston residents are accustomed to seeing their mayor on his early morning jogs up the East Battery, then on through downtown. It's a good way to keep tabs on his city. Riley recalls one particular morning:

> "I was jogging before sunup, when I saw Clarence. Clarence is a lifelong resident of Charleston. I've known him most of my life. He's an epileptic who lives with his mother, shines shoes for a living, and rides a bicycle to work. His epilepsy is advanced, and he frequently has spells. On this morning he was sitting on the wooden pier at Waterfront Park.

"A few weeks later, I ran into Clarence and asked if he goes there often. Clarence told me that he goes every day because it's so beautiful—that he likes watching the ships come in and seeing the sunrise."

"All people crave beauty," Riley says. "Beauty does not know any economic zones. Beauty makes people happy and if it's in the public realm, it enriches us because we own it." Therefore, making beautiful, meaningful places is a "moral imperative," according to Riley. We have to make them for the Clarences of the world. The only options Clarence has are in his city, says Riley. "He can't take a trip. And this is true for so many people—the city they live in is all they have. So when you create a beautiful place in the city for people in modest circumstances that gives them a sense of ownership, of belonging, you've made it worthwhile for everyone."

> IF WE ARE A NATION WHERE ALL THE FINEST ZONES ARE PRIVATELY OWNED, THEN WHAT WE OWN TOGETHER AS CITIZENS IS NOT VERY MUCH. THE GREATEST CITIES ARE THOSE WITH THE MOST BEAUTIFUL PUBLIC PLACES. JOSEPH P. RILEY, JR.

When Riley speaks of the moral imperative to create beautiful places in the city for all citizens to own and enjoy, he appeals to our best instincts. His impassioned belief takes on a spiritual dimension, recalling generations of gifted southern statesmen, past and present. Joe Riley knows that Waterfront Park is so valuable because it belongs to every citizen in Charleston. He says that the 20th century is mostly the century of the private zone, where we come together in private backyards, shopping malls, and gated communities; whereas the historic role of the city has been to celebrate the public zones that we share and own collectively. Great cities, he says, are those that "embrace the opportunity to enhance the beautiful and generous public realm—those zones and spaces and buildings so wonderfully owned by our people, the richest and the poorest, to the same degree."[iv]

NOTES

i Joseph P. Riley, Jr., "Caring for Cities" (Presentation at ULI meeting, Fall 2000).

ii Stephen Kinzer, "A Planned Museum Would Lead Charleston to Its Past," *New York Times,* August 14, 2001.

iii Joseph P. Riley, Jr., letter to Jaquelin Robertson, January 1985. Published in *Places,* Winter 1996, p. 8.

iv Joseph P. Riley, Jr., "Address to Annual Meeting of U.S. Conference of Mayors Following September 11," January 25, 2002. Published in *U.S. Mayor,* February 18, 2002.

PRIMARY REFERENCES

Agnew, David. "Joe Riley Offers Paradigm of Leadership." *The State,* March 18, 2001.

Hudnut, William H., III. "City Living: Mayors' Forum." *Urban Land,* July 2000.

Lundberg, Kirsten. "Mayor Joseph P. Riley, Charleston, South Carolina: The Politics of Preservation" (Case study C16-89-905.0). John F. Kennedy School of Government, Harvard University, 1989. Case study gives comprehensive background of Charleston Place development and related preservation issues.

Peirce, Neal. "Charleston's Master Designer." *Charlotte Observer*, January 4, 1994.

Riggs, Trisha. "Building on Success: The Pride of Joseph P. Riley, Jr." *Urban Land*, October 2000.

Riley, Joseph P., Jr. "Address to Annual Meeting of U.S. Conference of Mayors, January 25, 2002." *U.S. Mayor*, February 18, 2002.

Riley, Joseph P., Jr., and Jaquelin Robertson. "Introduction." *Places*, Winter 1996. This issue on mayors and city design discussed the Mayors' Institute on City Design.

Swope, Christopher. "Master of the Public Realm." *Governing*, November 2003.

AUTHOR INTERVIEWS

David Agnew, former executive assistant to Mayor Riley from 1996 to 2001, April 2004, by telephone.

Robert Campbell, FAIA , architecture critic, *Boston Globe*, April 2004, by telephone.

Yvonne Fortenberry, director of Design, Development & Preservation, City of Charleston, April 2004, by telephone.

John Hildreth, southeastern director, National Trust for Historic Preservation, April 2004, by telephone.

Michael Maher, director, Civic Design Center, City of Charleston, April 2004.

John Norquist, president and CEO, Congress for the New Urbanism, April 2004, by telephone.

Mayor Joseph P. Riley, Jr., April 2004.

Jaquelin Robertson, FAIA, AICP, partner, Cooper, Robertson & Partners, April 2004, by telephone.

Kitty Robertson, executive director, Historic Charleston Foundation, April 2004, by telephone.

Lawrence O. Thompson, executive assistant to Mayor Riley, City of Charleston, April 2004.

Vanessa Turner-Maybank, director, Office of Tourism Management, City of Charleston, April 2004.

Barbara W. Vaughn, director of Public Information, City of Charleston, April 2004.

HE BROUGHT TO HIS TASK LUMINOUS INTELLECT, PERSONAL
CONVICTION, DEEP HISTORICAL KNOWLEDGE, THE EYE OF AN ARTIST
AND THE PEN OF AN ANGEL, AND, ABOVE ALL, AN INCORRUPTIBLE
DEVOTION TO THE COMMON GOOD. JAMES Q. WILSON
FORMER SHATTUCK PROFESSOR OF GOVERNMENT
HARVARD UNIVERSITY

DANIEL PATRICK MOYNIHAN

STATESMAN OF THE PUBLIC REALM

DANIEL PATRICK MOYNIHAN always loved trains and was supremely bothered by the peeling paint of the scenic Hell's Gate Bridge that joins the New York boroughs of Queens and the Bronx. The grand old bridge had not been painted in more than half a century. Amtrak didn't care, but Moynihan did. The senior senator had enough clout with Amtrak and the U.S. Department of Transportation to get them to agree to paint the bridge in 1992. But first, he set up a color selection committee of esteemed designers and urbanists: architect David Childs, now lead designer of the Freedom Tower at the site of the World Trade Center; abstract painter Bob Wyman; president of the Municipal Art Society (MAS) Kent Barwick; and a husband-and-wife team of color consultants who had recently completed work on new galleries at the Metropolitan Museum of Art. After deliberating for several weeks, they finally agreed on a shade of maroon that reminded them of the color of the old Pennsylvania railroad cars. They sent a bucket of the maroon paint to the senator in Washington. "He said the color was absolutely perfect," notes Barwick.

> MOYNIHAN'S ACHIEVEMENTS ARE WORTHY OF THE GREAT PUBLIC BUILDERS, FROM HADRIAN TO GEORGES HAUSSMANN TO ROBERT MOSES, ONLY MOYNIHAN'S ARE HUMANE. ROBERT PECK, FORMER MOYNIHAN CHIEF OF STAFF AND FORMER COMMISSIONER OF PUBLIC BUILDINGS SERVICE OF THE U.S. GENERAL SERVICES ADMINISTRATION

Who else in Congress would have cared enough to get the bridge painted? Who else would have bothered to assemble a committee of design cognoscenti to select just the right hue?

Cities, architecture, and grand civic spaces were constant themes throughout Moynihan's career. The public square he loved best was the one he spent half a lifetime reviving.

FIXING UP THE NATION'S MAIN STREET

On the drive back from his inaugural in 1961, President Kennedy was dismayed at the shabby state of the nation's Avenue of the Presidents. Designed as the great ceremonial axis linking the White House and the Capitol—a physical symbol of the separate, but unified branches of the American government—Pennsylvania Avenue was lined on one side with monumental buff-colored limestone buildings in the neoclassic style. On the other side were mostly decrepit brick buildings with pawnshops, liquor stores, and peep stalls. Kennedy asked Arthur J. Goldberg, his secretary of labor, to do something about cleaning up the avenue. Goldberg formed a committee to look into construction of new federal office space and recommendations for reviving Pennsylvania Avenue. Daniel Patrick Moynihan, special assistant to Goldberg, was put in charge of writing the recommendations. So goes the legend.

When Daniel Patrick Moynihan joined President Kennedy's new administration in 1961 as special assistant to Secretary of Labor Goldberg, he had already earned a reputation as a politically inclined intellectual and urban expert. He had worked almost four years as an assistant to Governor Averell Harriman and had taught at Syracuse University. "Moynihan's first act of note on the national stage," says Robert Peck, who served as chief of staff to the senator, "was as a city planner." His ambitious proposal for reviving Pennsylvania Avenue was hitched at the end of the banal-sounding document, "Report to the President by the Ad Hoc Committee on Federal Office Space," issued in 1962. The strategy of burying the proposal in an appendix to a turgid report on government office space, along with a set of "Guiding Principles for Federal Architecture," has led some people, like Peck, to think that the whole thing, including the Kennedy legend, was a

Pennsylvania Avenue during John F. Kennedy's inaugural parade in January 1961.

COURTESY OF THE HISTORY PLACE

Moynihan invention. Peck believes that Moynihan was so loyal to the memory of Kennedy that he credited the president with the idea of fixing up Pennsylvania Avenue.[i]

NO OFFICIAL STYLE

However it happened, Moynihan turned what many would have treated as a routine assignment into an opportunity to establish federal architectural policy. "The belief that good design is optional, or in some way separate from the question of the provision of office space itself, does not bear scrutiny," he wrote with his trademark vigor. His first directive was to be contemporary: "avoid an official style." Government buildings should embody the "finest contemporary architectural thought." At that time, the federal government, according to Moynihan, had built scarcely a contemporary building in Washington in two generations. He knew, however, that recognizing the contemporary architecture of the time did not guarantee excellence. "There are great moments in architecture, there are lesser moments. But we wouldn't miss any."[ii]

CAROL M. HIGHSMITH PHOTOGRAPHY

Pennsylvania Avenue today—after Senator Moynihan devoted half his life to its revival.

Moynihan's proposal for reviving Pennsylvania Avenue traced the history of the architecture of the nation's capital, starting with the original plans of Major Charles Pierre L'Enfant, in which the grand axis of Pennsylvania Avenue—connecting the separate branches of government—was to be the main thoroughfare of the city of Washington. Instead, Moynihan noted, "It remains a vast, unformed, cluttered expanse at the heart of the Nation's Capital," and the main court of the Federal Triangle (the Depression had stopped construction to complete the Triangle) was left to become a parking lot of "unsurpassed ugliness."[iii]

In the Ad Hoc Committee report, Moynihan worried that the Capitol itself was "cut off from the most developed part of the city by a blighted area that is unsightly by day and empty by night." Large sections on the north side of the street were decayed beyond repair; many buildings would have to be replaced. Moynihan saw this as a great opportunity that might "not come again for a half century or more."

So began Moynihan's stewardship of rebuilding Pennsylvania Avenue, which would take nearly the rest of his life. One would assume that a proposal for redeveloping Pennsylvania Avenue, which was tacked onto a report to alleviate the shortage of federal office space, would endorse, not criticize, extending the Federal Triangle's phalanx of efficient office buildings along the north edge of the avenue. But Moynihan's recommendations reached far beyond a simple request for new office space. His ambitious proposal called for creating a lively mix of shops, offices, and housing, along with theaters and other arts facilities and great civic spaces that would be developed jointly by public and private interests.

The government had not built significant office space in Washington since the Federal Triangle buildings, which ended with the 1929 crash. Like most other federal agencies in the 1960s, the labor department was scattered in numerous buildings throughout the city. It was anticipated that the underdeveloped parts of the avenue would be turned into office space for federal workers. But Moynihan was concerned about isolating the Capitol, which he knew would happen if the north side were to be lined, like the south side of the avenue, with only office buildings that emptied out after 6:00 p.m. He envisioned more diverse mixed-use development, including housing, for the north side of Pennsylvania Avenue. This mixed-use concept, which Moynihan believed would enliven the city, was exceptionally urban for the time.

GUIDING PRINCIPLES FOR FEDERAL ARCHITECTURE

In the course of its consideration of the general subject of Federal office space, the committee has given some thought to the need for a set of principles which will guide the Government in the choice of design for Federal buildings. The committee takes it to be a matter of general understanding that the economy and suitability of Federal office space derive directly from the architectural design. The belief that good design is optional or in some way separate from the question of the provision of office space itself does not bear scrutiny, and in fact invites the least efficient use of public money.

The design of Federal office buildings, particularly those to be located in the nation's capital, must meet a twofold requirement. First, it must provide efficient and economical facilities for the use of Government agencies. Second, it must provide visual testimony to the dignity, enterprise, vigor, and stability of the American Government.

It should be our object to meet the test of Pericles's evocation to the Athenians, which the President commended to the Massachusetts legislature in his address on January 9, 1961: "We do not imitate—for we are a model to others."

The committee is also of the opinion that the Federal Government, no less than other public and private organizations concerned with the construction of new buildings, should take advantage of the increasingly fruitful collaboration between architecture and the fine arts.

With these objects in view, the committee recommends a three-point architectural policy for the Federal Government.

An informal President's Advisory Council on Pennsylvania Avenue was set up to carry out the proposal, cochaired by Moynihan and Nathaniel Owings, from the San Francisco office of Skidmore, Owings & Merrill—then, as now, one of the country's largest commercial architecture firms. By this time, Goldberg had moved onto the Supreme Court, leaving Moynihan in charge of Pennsylvania Avenue. Owings assembled some of the country's most notable design experts—Douglas Haskell, editor of *Architectural Forum,* and architects Paul Thiry, master of the Seattle World's Fair, and Minoru Yamasaki, designer of the World Trade Center. "It was a very exciting time in Washington," said Moynihan. "You didn't have to have an executive order to start up a committee on Pennsylvania Avenue. You just did it. Of course, it was waiting to happen."[iv]

PENNSYLVANIA AVENUE SHOULD BE LIVELY, FRIENDLY, AND INVITING, AS WELL AS DIGNIFIED AND IMPRESSIVE. IT SHOULD BE A STREET ON WHICH IT WOULD BE PLEASANT TO WALK AS WELL AS POSSIBLE TO DRIVE. "REPORT TO THE PRESIDENT BY THE AD HOC COMMITTEE ON FEDERAL OFFICE SPACE," 1962

1. The policy shall be to provide requisite and adequate facilities in an architectural style and form which is distinguished and which will reflect the dignity, enterprise, vigor, and stability of the American National Government. Major emphasis should be placed on the choice of designs that embody the finest contemporary American architectural thought. Specific attention should be paid to the possibilities of incorporating into such designs qualities which reflect the regional architectural traditions of that part with emphasis on the work of living American artists. Designs shall adhere to sound construction practice and utilize materials, methods, and equipment of proven dependability. Buildings shall be economical to build, operate, and maintain, and should be accessible to the handicapped.

2. The development of an official style must be avoided. Design must flow from the architectural profession to the Government and not vice versa. The Government should be willing to pay some additional cost to avoid excessive uniformity in design of Federal buildings. Competitions for the design of Federal buildings may be held where appropriate. The advice of distinguished architects ought to, as a rule, be sought prior to the award of important design contracts.

3. The choice and development of the building site should be considered the first step of the design process. This choice should be made in cooperation with local agencies. Special attention should be paid to the general ensemble of streets and public places of which Federal buildings will form a part. Where possible, buildings should be located so as to permit a generous development of landscape.[v]

 is the caption below (within image region): text on the vertical edge reads "COURTESY, DAVID CHILDS, SOM, NEW YORK OFFICE"

Hardly anyone knows, says Peck, that Moynihan also wanted to deploy a concert hall, theater, and opera house at points along the avenue to animate it. Apparently, there had long been talk of creating a national cultural center in Washington. President Kennedy asked Moynihan and his colleagues to present this idea, along with plans for redeveloping the avenue, to congressional leaders on his return from Dallas. But tragedy interfered.

On November 22, 1963, Moynihan was at a lunch meeting in Georgetown to discuss the upcoming presentation when they received a phone call that the President had been shot. Devastated by the loss of this man he so greatly admired but hadn't yet gotten to know, Moynihan lamented, "I guess there's no point in being Irish if you don't know that the world is going to break your heart eventually." vi

President Nixon with a model of Pennsylvania Avenue.

When Jacqueline Kennedy left the White House, Lyndon Johnson asked what he could do for her. She asked him to continue work on Pennsylvania Avenue. President Johnson accepted the report of the advisory council and reformed the council in 1965 as the Temporary Commission on Pennsylvania Avenue. But the plan languished during the next several years. By this time, Moynihan had left Washington for a stint in academia—first at Wesleyan University's Center for Advanced Studies, then at Harvard, where he was director of Harvard's and the Massachusetts Institute of Technology's Joint Center for Urban Studies.

Meanwhile, David Childs, a promising young architect who would become Moynihan's lifelong friend, came to Washington to design the Woodrow Wilson International School for Scholars, which was to be built on Pennsylvania Avenue. "The idea," says Childs, "was to create a scholarly institution with housing for its fellows, much like the American Academy in Rome." But Childs worried that his project, along with the plan for the avenue, had never been officially approved by Congress, and might never be built.

All that changed, notes Childs, when Nixon was elected president in 1968 and appointed Moynihan his assistant for urban affairs. Moynihan returned to Washington and resumed his stewardship of the Pennsylvania Avenue redevelopment effort, then directly under his aegis.

"Moynihan's return made all the difference in the world," says Childs, "for now we had someone working on the inside. As Pat used to say, every night he would pull the information on Pennsylvania Avenue from the bottom of the pile on George Schultz's [director of the Office of Management and Budget under Nixon] desk and place it on top. That way we became known in the White House and gained credibility."[vii]

Moynihan knew it was important to get congressional approval for the redevelopment plan. But first, he wanted to revise it. "Although the new plan was based largely on the original," observes Childs, "we had learned a great deal about creating livelier streets and more animated urban spaces, and Pat was very much a part of that. We removed the network of skywalks and pedestrian bridges in the first plan that would have pulled activity from the streets," he explains. "Then we designed a much smaller plaza at the western terminus." As Moynihan would write later about his good friend Nat Owings, he "did dearly love a grand vista. . . . [That] got him into planning some plazas the size of which would have given the Renaissance pause and reminded more than a few Washingtonians what the summer heat is like."[viii]

The earlier plan reflected the urban renewal mentality of the time and the experience of some early commission members like Chloethiel Woodard Smith, who had designed the wholesale renewal of southwest Washington, D.C. Some members wanted to start practically from scratch and build a completely new avenue. The first plan also called for tearing down a number of grand old buildings, including the Willard Hotel and the Old Post Office Building.

THE STRENGTH OF THE NEW, REVISED PLAN WAS THE PUBLIC REALM. ALTHOUGH THE REBUILDING ON THE AVENUE WAS TO BE AN ARCHITECTURAL LABORATORY REFLECTING CURRENT DESIGN TASTE, IT WAS THE SPACE BETWEEN THE BUILDINGS THAT PAT ESPECIALLY CARED ABOUT. AND THAT'S, IN MY MIND, WHERE PENNSYLVANIA AVENUE HAD ITS GREATEST SUCCESSES. DAVID CHILDS, ARCHITECT

But it soon became clear that it would be much too costly to acquire almost the entire stretch of street on the north side, as envisioned in the early clearance plan. Moreover, design tastes and attitudes on preserving historic buildings had changed since the first commission began its work. Each successive plan for the avenue, notes Bob Peck, was a bit less monolithic, a bit more urban.

Childs explains that the buildings on the avenue edges were intended as liners for the great barrel of space that links each end of the axis. The liner buildings are interesting, much like the buildings along the Champs Elysées, but they are part of the course; whereas the Capitol and the White House, which he describes as the "divas singing the arias," are the great pieces of urban sculpture at each end of the avenue. A primary purpose of the Pennsylvania Avenue Development Corporation (PADC) was to create the great civic spaces that would encourage private sector investment in the area.

President Nixon eventually heard the presentation on the revised plan and with Moynihan, he took a walking tour of the avenue. Nixon endorsed the plan and personally lobbied Congress on behalf of a quasi-government development agency with vast powers of purchasing land and raising bond revenues. Not until 1972 did Congress pass enabling legislation to create the Pennsylvania Avenue Development Corporation, the financial engine with condemnation powers and the power to borrow from the Treasury that would get the job done.

Toward the end of the Nixon administration, Moynihan was named a delegate to the United Nations and later appointed ambassador to India, after which he served a year as U.S. representative to the United Nations. In 1976, he won the open seat as junior senator of New York, which he held for four six-year terms, and during which he resumed his squireship of Pennsylvania Avenue. Throughout his career in the Senate, Moynihan was the strongest ally in Congress for the PADC and its work to regenerate the avenue. Completion of the Federal Triangle with the addition of the Ronald Reagan Building and International Trade Center in the mid-1990s was accomplished primarily through his interest and influence.

LIVING ABOVE THE SQUARE

The redevelopment of this former department store into apartments was one of the first residential projects in the burgeoning Penn Quarter neighborhood.

While Moynihan and Childs were working in the early 1970s on the plan to resuscitate Pennsylvania Avenue, cities in the United States were emptying out. This was especially true in Washington. The 1968 riots following the assassination of Martin Luther King, Jr., swept areas north of Pennsylvania Avenue, but the consequences reverberated throughout the central business district. Shoppers fled to the suburban shopping malls that sprang up around the Beltway, and downtown businesses followed. Many banks had redlined the area around the avenue. Between 1960 and 1969, the Pennsylvania Avenue corridor suffered a 42 percent loss of business.[ix] By the early 1970s, numerous vacant buildings dotted the avenue. Private businesses abandoned downtown D.C. and moved west to Georgetown or the West End.

CAROL M. HIGHSMITH PHOTOGRAPHY

Despite all this, Moynihan, and especially Nat Owings, pressed for housing and cultural and arts facilities to keep the area alive at night. David Childs says that Moynihan understood that to animate our urban places, we need people walking on the sidewalks to make the area safe and appealing. To do this, housing and restaurants and theaters were of the utmost necessity.

Housing had always been a part of the early planning for the avenue. But apart from Nat and Pat, says Childs, no one else on the commission cared much about it. Remember, this was a time when anyone who was anybody in Washington lived in Georgetown or Cleveland Park. The idea of attracting middle- and upper-income residents to the area seemed absurd. There certainly was a void to fill. A congressional survey in the early 1970s found only 13 housing units in the entire Pennsylvania Avenue corridor.ˣ

It would take almost 20 years after the PADC was formed to get the first new housing built on the avenue. Jay Brodie, who had directed Baltimore's Department of Housing and Community Development, was hired as the new PADC executive director to jumpstart housing on the avenue. Brodie recalls that when he first joined the PADC in 1984, area banks agreed that there was a market for hotels and offices, but they balked when it came to financing housing, especially market-rate housing. Many people predicted that housing would fail. So Market Square—an office building with shops and restaurants meeting the sidewalk and luxury condominiums on the top floors—"was the critical leading edge of the housing," notes Brodie. As the first mixed-use residential development built under the plan, Brodie says, "It was essential that it be well designed, well marketed, and successful if the avenue were to be a viable housing option for people."

The senator and his wife were among the first new residents on Pennsylvania Avenue with the opening of Market Square, a mixed-use complex with retail, office, and luxury condominiums on the top floors.

Senator Moynihan and his wife were among the first residents at Market Square when they moved there in 1990. They joined two units and later purchased a third. "We couldn't have had a better marketing couple," recalls Brodie. From their 700-square-foot terrace, the Moynihans enjoyed sweeping views of the Treasury Building and White House to the west and the Capitol to the east.

[MARKET SQUARE] IS AS CLOSE AS WE GOT TO THE NAT OWINGS ORIGINAL ITALIAN HILL TOWN DREAM, EVEN IF THE RED TILE ROOFTOPS WE LOOK OUT ON ARE THOSE OF THE FEDERAL TRIANGLE BUILDINGS. BUT NAT WOULD HAVE LOVED IT! ELIZABETH MOYNIHAN

The new Market Square residence became "Washington's beachfront property," says Jo-Ann Neuhaus, who was one of the first staff members at the PADC. Sales were so brisk that the units in the second twin building, Market Square East, originally planned as rentals, were sold instead as condominiums. The success of these two early housing developments paved the way for many more residential developments in what has become the very urbane Pennsylvania Quarter—

brimming with restaurants, shops, theaters, and museums—one of Washington's premier downtown neighborhoods.

Brodie's strategy of following up Market Square with a variety of housing choices—rentals, for-sale units, rehabbed historic buildings, new construction, small studios, and large loft spaces—paid off. When he started work on the avenue, Moynihan told a *Washington Post* reporter that no one could call the area a slum, since "no one lived there." Although a few small apartments had been built above some stores on the avenue, practically no one had lived in the area for one hundred years. Today, the neighborhood has approximately 1,165 residences with another thousand units in the pipeline, says Neuhaus, who serves now as executive director of the Penn Quarter Neighborhood.

COMPLETING THE FEDERAL TRIANGLE

By far the toughest development parcel on the avenue was the last unbuilt site of the Federal Triangle that would become the Ronald Reagan Building and International Trade Center. The parcel, much of which was a vast parking lot, was controlled by the U.S. General Services Administration, headed by Terry Golden, a former partner with the Dallas development firm Trammell Crow. As Moynihan described it, Golden "saw $2 billion worth of real estate being used as a parking lot and said, No, that doesn't make sense."[xi] It was Golden's idea to combine an international center for trade and technology—a concept that had been discussed for several years—with additional federal office space. Moynihan liked the concept, but was concerned that GSA had no experience with complicated, public/private developments of this scale. So he rewrote the legislation and placed PADC in the lead.

The last unbuilt site of the Federal Triangle was a vast parking lot that was transformed into the Ronald Reagan Building and International Trade Center.

CAROL M. HIGHSMITH PHOTOGRAPHY

The international trade complex, with a floor space equivalent to two-thirds that of the Pentagon, was fraught with difficulties from the start. Some people objected that the plan didn't fit in with the overall concept of the Federal Triangle. The vast number of government reviewing agencies was staggering. Once it became evident that Wall Street would not finance the development, GSA staked out a difficult position and pressed hard to eliminate most of the mixed-use elements, according to Jay Brodie.

"Sure there were compromises," acknowledges Brodie. One was the original plan for two theaters. The cost got too high so they were trimmed back. "Moynihan," he says, "was called upon regularly to referee such clashes. He understood the cost problem, that prices typically rise over the course of large development projects, but he refused to throw out the essential vision."

GUIDING PRINCIPLES ENDURE

"Guiding Principles for Federal Architecture"— "this peculiarly American, anti-official declaration about official architecture," as described by Bob Peck, lives on. Maybe the one-page declaration has lasted for the reason that Moynihan so often observed: because it is "unbureaucratically brief." Or maybe because it is absolutely fundamental. Charles Atherton, secretary of Washington's Commission of Fine Arts, compares the "Guiding Principles . . . [to] the Declaration of Independence. You can't revise them. They are so basic and so right in everything."[xii]

The "Guiding Principles" received new vigor from the GSA's "Design Excellence Program," created in 1994 by Edward Feiner, chief architect of the Public Buildings Service of GSA, to overhaul the way in which the federal government makes architecture. Coincidentally, Feiner's boss during the early years of the Design Excellence program was Bob Peck, who served as commissioner of the Public Buildings Service from 1995 to 2001. The program, according to Reed Kroloff, former editor of *Architecture* magazine, "streamlined a notoriously burdensome application process and injected it with a new-found respect for the value of a firm's design reputation. Consequently, many architects—among them signature designers like Richard Meier and Thom Mayne—are now competing for government projects that previously they would never have considered."[xiii]

Moynihan must have beamed when he saw the plans for the Newseum, which was to be located across from the National Gallery and next to the Canadian Embassy. It was the last piece of the more than 40-year buildout on Pennsylvania Avenue. Although the museum is not a federal building and, therefore, need not follow the "Guiding Principles for Federal Architecture," the striking, contemporary design by Polshek Partnership realizes Moynihan's vision to line the north side of the avenue with mixed-use development that is "lively, friendly, inviting," as well as dignified. Architect James Stewart Polshek equates transparency

WITHOUT SENATOR MOYNIHAN'S INCREDIBLE PERSISTENCE AND LEADERSHIP, WE WOULD HAVE ENDED UP WITH ONLY AN OFFICE BUILDING. BUT HE RECOGNIZED THAT TO BUILD JUST ANOTHER OFFICE BUILDING ON THIS UNIQUE SITE, ONLY TWO BLOCKS FROM THE WHITE HOUSE, WOULD BE AN INCREDIBLE WASTE. SO HE PUSHED TO KEEP THE CORE MIXED-USE VISION. THE ATRIUM, THE FOOD COURT, AND THE TUNNEL BENEATH 14TH STREET, ALL COSTLY ITEMS, WOULD NOT BE HERE TODAY IF MOYNIHAN HADN'T FOUGHT FOR THEM.

M. JAY BRODIE, FORMER EXECUTIVE DIRECTOR, PENNSYLVANIA AVENUE DEVELOPMENT CORPORATION

"Moynihan Place" on Pennsylvania Avenue and 13th Street has a pylon with the "Guiding Principles for Federal Architecture" on it.

DAVID HAWXHURST, PHOTOGRAPHER; COURTESY WOODROW WILSON CENTER

Now under construction on Pennsylvania Avenue across from the National Gallery of Art, the Newseum celebrates the First Amendment.

with democracy and made this the metaphor for the building, which celebrates the First Amendment. Now under construction, the museum complex has a 4,500-square-foot window in the Pennsylvania Avenue facade that will give passersby views of galleries, a soaring central atrium, and a giant media screen that will project breaking news.

NOT FOR THE SHORT-WINDED

Moynihan remembered writing Jacqueline Kennedy to say that they had just gotten the legislation that authorized building the International Trade Center site. "I got back the most beautiful three-page letter saying 25 years is a long time not to give up on something. She never did." [xiv] Neither did Moynihan. He understood that worthwhile endeavors take a long time, that city building and rebuilding are tasks that must withstand multiple changes in political administrations. His work on Pennsylvania Avenue stretched through eight presidential terms.

CITY PLANNING IS A LONG PROCESS, AND IT REQUIRES A MEASURE OF COMMITMENT THAT IS NOT LIKELY TO BE SUSTAINED UNLESS THERE IS SOME GRASP OF THIS AT THE OUTSET. THIS IS ESPECIALLY SO IN OUR AGE . . . [WHERE] IT HAS BECOME EVER MORE DIFFICULT TO MAKE LARGE PLANS AND CARRY THEM THROUGH. DANIEL PATRICK MOYNIHAN

Although Moynihan understood the need for long-term planning, he was famously impatient with the increasingly cumbersome public approval processes. When Frederick Papert, president of the 42nd Street Development Corporation, wrote Senator Moynihan in 1991 asking his support for the 42nd Street trolley, which would replace the street's crosstown buses (the consultant studies had all been completed), Moynihan responded: "Twelve years, eleven studies, and $2 million in consultant fees and the city is ready to move. Perhaps." [xv]

Dismayed at the torpid pace of the trolley project, to which Moynihan gave his support, he told Papert he sometimes "longed for the days when Boss Croker could build the IRT [New York's subway] as a favor for a friend."

EYE OF AN ARTIST

Liz Moynihan says that her husband was not artistic in the usual sense—he didn't paint or draw—but "he had a wonderful eye." She recounts the many descriptive letters he wrote when he studied as a Fulbright fellow at the London School of Economics, letters filled with impressions of the architecture and cities he visited in Europe. Yet it was politics that brought Liz and Pat together when they met working in Governor Averell Harriman's office in the mid-1950s. Besides politics, they also shared a passion for art and architecture. After they married, Liz studied sculpture and the history of architecture and landscape architecture. She grew interested in India's Mughal gardens when her husband was ambassador to India, and wrote scholarly articles on the subject.

Moynihan has said that his interest in architecture started in his youth, when he would walk by the majestic buildings of Manhattan, buildings like Raymond Hood's art deco McGraw-Hill tower.[xvi] Later in life, architect friends including David Childs and Nat Owings had a great influence on Moynihan. "Despite the great age difference, Nat and Pat were extraordinarily close, like brothers," says David Childs. "There was a magic between them. They shared a marvelous sense of humor and irreverent wit, and they held the same strong conviction about the need for communal life in our cities."

Moynihan recounted the time he and Nat climbed the 265-foot tower of the abandoned Old Post Office Building at Pennsylvania Avenue and 12th Street to enjoy the "stunning panorama of the whole of the city. On at least three occasions that I recall, Nat Owings and I risked, if not our lives, then surely our reputations, ascending an endless Piranesian fantasia of rickety catwalks and dung-layered spiral staircases, only to break out onto that startling view." [xvii]

David Childs's close friendship with Moynihan started when Moynihan returned to Washington in 1968 to work for President Nixon. It was the transition period; Moynihan's family still lived in Cambridge. "Pat was in the White House and I worked next door in an office in the Old Executive Office Building. We met often for dinner and would talk late into the night. We lived and breathed urbanism, especially Pennsylvania Avenue."

Famous for his strong, fearless opinions about buildings, Moynihan introduced a 1981 Senate resolution to "put the plastic covering back on" the newly finished Hart Senate Office, a "building whose banality is exceeded only by its expense." Neither did he care for the design of the 1960s Jacob Javits Federal Building in Foley Square. During its dedication, he was heard to say, "Just a pity that we named the ugliest building in the city for Jake Javits." And in a Public Works Committee hearing to fund roof repairs for the Kennedy Center, Moynihan noted that the architect, Edward Durrell

Senator Moynihan with his wife Elizabeth at their farm in Pindars Corner, in upstate New York.

COURTESY MOYNIHAN FAMILY

COURTESY MOYNIHAN FAMILY

The senator enjoying
Central Park.

Stone, had also designed the U.S. Embassy in New Delhi, which bore a strong resemblance to the Kennedy Center, as did many of Stone's buildings. Moynihan had personal knowledge that the embassy's roof also leaked, as did the Stone-designed government building in Albany, where Moynihan had worked many years before. He said that Stone reminded him of the character Mr. Kremlin in the Benjamin Disraeli novel *Sibyl,* who is "described as someone 'distinguished for ignorance' as he had but one idea and it was wrong."[xviii]

GETTING ON THE POLITICAL AGENDA

Kent Barwick, president of the Municipal Art Society in New York, credits Moynihan with laying the groundwork for preservation and planning advocacy in New York. Barwick recalls a memorable raw, rainy day in the fall of 1968 when Moynihan traveled from Boston to speak at a conference in New York on saving the South Street Seaport Fulton Market. Moynihan, who was teaching at Harvard then, spoke about working with President Kennedy on the cleanup of Pennsylvania Avenue. He noted that Kennedy didn't truly comprehend the full importance of the redevelopment effort, but he liked Moynihan's ideas and let him have his way as a favor. "But getting what you want as a matter of grace only takes you so far," Moynihan continued. "If you really want to get someplace, you have to get on the political agenda. You need to organize, line up voters, and make certain your agenda is taken seriously by elected officials."

"This was practical politics 101 from a great teacher," says Barwick. Moynihan's message hit home. "New York's planning and preservation advocacy movement owes a great deal to the good advice of the young professor on that blustery, rainy day," notes Barwick.

When he returned to politics, Moynihan became a master at getting his favorite projects on the political agenda, several of which were train stations.

RESTORING THE GRANDEUR

In his interview to work for Senator Moynihan, Bob Peck was told that his first project would be to fix up Washington's Union Station. The senator's office was in the Dirksen Senate Office Building, just a couple of blocks from Union Station. The debacle started when the federal government decided to turn Daniel Burnham's beaux arts masterpiece into a visitors center for the Bicentennial celebration. But they were in such a rush that the roof was not repaired and it leaked badly.

The new visitors center, with a mean little shack of a train station behind the main building, was a disaster from the beginning. No one wanted to visit the dark pit with the huge slide show of the Capitol dome when they could view the real thing across the street. And the building had literally gone to seed. Peck recounts that at a hearing, Moynihan asked an official with the Department of the Interior about taking a count to make sure the number of people who exited the pit was the same as the number that entered.[xix] As a result of the leaky roof, giant mushrooms grew on the floor inside and large plaster chunks started falling, so that the National Park Service eventually closed the building. The enormously costly boondoggle, the subject of several exposés by the CBS *60 Minutes* show, was a great source of embarrassment to everyone.

Moynihan, Jacqueline Onassis, and Joan Mondale celebrate the victory over saving Grand Central Station.

When Senator Moynihan spoke of his plans to introduce a bill to revitalize Union Station, "I advised him not to," says Peck. "The building was a complete disaster and no one wanted to be connected with it. I told him he'd be ridiculed for introducing a bill calling for any more federal involvement in the building. We needed to figure out another way." Of course, the senator marched down to the floor the next day and introduced the bill to revitalize Union Station. Independent to the bone, Moynihan didn't care much whether people liked the idea. But he knew it was insane to allow this magnificent building to languish.

So Moynihan and Peck worked with staff on the Senate Environment and Public Works Committee to create a public/private redevelopment corporation to return the building to its original grandeur and use as a train station. The mixed-use strategy—of incorporating private stores and a variety of good restaurants—succeeded beyond everyone's wildest dreams. The relatively quick turnaround—the building reopened as a train station in 1986—was deemed a huge success.

Moynihan and many others never got over the tragedy of New York's Penn Station, when McKim, Mead & White's beaux arts masterpiece was torn down in 1963 to make way for the new Madison Square Garden and an office complex. The railroad station portion was buried in the basement corridor and the shards of the building were carted away to a landfill in New Jersey. Moynihan was fond of quoting the description of Vincent Scully, the well-known art historian, who in his book *American Architecture and Urbanism* wrote, "Through it [Penn Station] one entered the city like a god. One scuttles in now like a rat."

NEW YORK TIMES

Senator Moynihan presents the model of Moynihan Station—the reborn Penn Station—to President Clinton.

Destruction of Penn Station led to the passage of New York's landmarks law in 1965. Three years later, the owners of Grand Central Station proposed building an office tower above the terminal, which triggered a ten-year fight that ended with the 1978 U.S. Supreme Court ruling upholding the terminal's landmark status.

When he heard the court's decision that Grand Central was saved, Moynihan cheered: "We let Pennsylvania Station disappear in the Jersey marshes. We let ourselves go broke. We let a lot of things go to hell. But, by God, all that is behind us. There is nothing we can't do when we really are as good as we know how to be."

It is another train terminal that promises to be one of Moynihan's greatest contributions to the urban realm, according to architecture critic Paul Goldberger. It was Moynihan who thought of the idea to convert the old Farley Post Office into a reconstituted Penn Station. He spent the last decade of his life realizing this grand vision.

The U.S. General Post Office building, which had been designed by McKim, Mead & White as a companion building to Penn Station, opened in 1914 on Eighth Avenue across from the station. Beneath the postal building are tracks and platforms that extend and expand what is left of Penn Station. In the 1990s, the federal government built a modern mail-handling facility several blocks to the south of the post office building, where apart from the front retail lobby, most of the space was unused.

Moynihan gained the support of New York's Mayor David Dinkins who endorsed the conversion of the old Farley Post Office into Penn Station. To help fund the project, Amtrak and its development associates turned to Moynihan. That he had risen by this time to the position of chairman of the Finance Committee, through which all tax bills flow, notes *New Yorker* writer Sidney Blumenthal, meant that this project—re-creating an aboveground Penn Station—got people's attention. The senator fought mightily to realize his dream.

As was his way with other highly ambitious projects, Moynihan pushed relentlessly. He seized every opportunity to move the Penn Station project onto the political agenda. President Clinton said it was impossible to be with Moynihan without the senator bringing up the subject of his beloved Penn Station. Immediately following Dinkins's defeat, Moynihan inquired at the White

House about the future of Penn Station. He was asked to brief Clinton people about the project. His legendary persuasive powers worked. The President's budget contained some $100 million for the Pennsylvania Station Redevelopment Project. The rest of the money would come from a consortium of state, city, and transit interests.

THE SENATOR WANTED ME TO UNDERSTAND HOW THINGS GOT ACCOMPLISHED IN NEW YORK. HE TOLD ME MARVELOUS STORIES ABOUT WORKING ON HARRIMAN'S STAFF AND THE TIMES ROBERT MOSES WOULD MARCH INTO THE OFFICE AND HAND HARRIMAN AN ENVELOPE WITH A LIST OF PROJECTS HE WANTED TO GET DONE. AND THEY GOT DONE. ALEXANDROS WASHBURN, ARCHITECT

A young architect, Alexandros Washburn, who had once served as Moynihan's public works adviser, was put in charge of the Pennsylvania Station Development Corporation—a sister corporation to the Lower Manhattan Redevelopment Corporation, which is overseeing the rebuilding of Ground Zero. Moynihan's longtime friend David Childs would lead the station design for Skidmore, Owings & Merrill.

Moynihan met frequently with Washburn in New York to discuss the project. The vision for the reborn Penn Station, to be named "Moynihan Station," is both arrival and revival of what was once the grand entryway to the city. "The project is freighted with enormous civic intent," says Washburn. "How do you express this vision of arrival/revival as a piece of architecture? How do you take this tangle of tracks long buried beneath Madison Square Garden and make a traveler feel once again like he is entering the city as a god? How do you fund it as a piece of politics? How do you motivate three different government entities, city, state, and federal, plus the postal service—all with different priorities—to spend millions of dollars on realizing this vision?" These were the issues that Moynihan discussed with his young protégé.

Just as David Childs started his architectural career working on the redevelopment plan for Pennsylvania Avenue, so did he work with Moynihan many years later on the design of one of the greatest civic projects of his career. "Pat was my greatest adviser and supporter," says Childs. Although the Farley Post Office and Penn Station were designed as companion buildings, "they were totally different building types," says Childs. Childs's design retains the postal retail lobby and ceremonial rooms and creates the great arrival hall for the terminal that stretches two blocks behind the original building. "When I first showed the model to Moynihan and peeled away the roof segment

The vision for the new Moynihan Station is both arrival and revival of what was once the grand entryway to New York City.

RENDERING BY SOM, NEW YORK OFFICE

to display the enormous volumetric, two-dimensional truss that runs across the back of the building to create this great Baths-of-Caracalla space, there was dead silence. Finally Moynihan spoke. 'It's perfect. Now let's build it.'"

WHAT WE CONSERVE IS WHAT WE VALUE

Besides landmark train stations, Moynihan helped rescue and renew many other historic treasures, including Louis Sullivan's Guaranty Building in Buffalo and Cass Gilbert's Custom House at Bowling Green in New York City. Many notable buildings in Washington, including the Old Pension Building (now the National Building Museum), the Old Post Office Building, and the Willard Hotel on Pennsylvania Avenue, also benefited from his attention.

Historic preservation, for Moynihan, was a direct expression of our fundamental values. "What we conserve," he said, "says something about what we value." xx He noted that when traveling in foreign countries, people usually visit the great buildings and memorable civic spaces—the museums, the churches, the grand boulevards. These are the memories that endure. What will future generations say of our civilization as they look back on our convention centers, sports arenas, and shopping malls? Do we not want to be remembered for something more?

Kent Barwick never forgot the important lesson about getting on the political agenda that he learned many years ago from the young Harvard professor. Under Barwick's leadership, the Municipal Art Society organized a rally in Times Square to protest an early redevelopment plan that would have removed the giant illuminated billboards and turned the neighborhood into another office district. Moynihan gave lip service to the revitalization plan, which was backed by the Democratic mayor and governor, "but he knew in his heart that turning Times Square into another Wall Street or Park Avenue was a stupid thing to do," says Barwick.

To show what Times Square would be like without the jazzy colors and neon zip of the giant electric signs, the MAS turned out all the lights on the night of the rally. Everyone was instructed to wear a sailor's hat, to recall the famous photograph of the sailor kissing his girl in Times Square at the end of World War II. Senator Moynihan showed up in his sailor's hat.

LEADERSHIP OF IDEAS

What is unusual for a politician, says Bob Peck, is that Moynihan's "brand of leadership was one of ideas." For more than a generation, Moynihan occupied simultaneously the two worlds of ideas and politics and nourished both of them, observes Robert Katzmann, a former Moynihan teaching fellow at Harvard and now a federal judge, who organized a celebration and the Festschrift that followed, *Daniel Patrick Moynihan: The Intellectual in Public Life.*

When Moynihan died at the age of 76, a *Washington Post* editorial said that he had "pursued with distinction enough careers for half a dozen men of lesser talents and imagination: politician, presidential adviser, diplomat, author, professor, public intellectual." Moynihan's myriad interests—in cities and urban affairs, civic design, social security, sociology, welfare reform, auto safety, transportation, foreign relations, international law, and government secrecy—earned him the reputation of gadfly or renaissance man. But everyone agrees that Moynihan did not arrive at his opinions casually.

Time after time, Moynihan demonstrated that he had studied the issues firsthand. People on his staff say that he always looked to the primary sources; he refused to accept someone else's interpretation of the information. People admired his nimble, nuanced intellect and marveled at his ability to assimilate great quantities of complicated information and make sense of it all. Katzmann described his mind as "a great lending library."

David Childs recounts the time when the Temporary Commission on Pennsylvania Avenue was hard at work on its final plan to present to President Nixon. Moynihan asked the commission members to synthesize their concepts. But no one could agree. Meanwhile, Moynihan, said Childs, looked more and more depressed as the date for presenting the plan grew closer. With only two days before Nixon was to hear the presentation, notes Childs, Moynihan left the discussion group, crossed the room to his elderly Smith-Corona typewriter, and started typing at gunfire speed. He wrote the plan that President Nixon approved.

Unlike many congressional members, who rely mostly on staff to write speeches, articles, and letters, Moynihan did much of his own writing. He wrote eloquently and demanded the same from his staff. If he didn't like a piece of writing done by one of his staff, he was known to respond, "You wouldn't last a week at the *New York Times.*" Bob Peck said they once timed him. It took Moynihan less than ten minutes to turn out an eloquent two-page statement for the press.

CAROL M. HIGHSMITH PHOTOGRAPHY

CAROL M. HIGHSMITH PHOTOGRAPHY

Senator Moynihan helped rescue many historic treasures in Washington, D.C., including the Old Post Office building and the Willard Hotel, both on Pennsylvania Avenue.

Moynihan authored more than 15 books, many of which he wrote at his farm in Pindars Corners in upstate New York. Peck observes that Moynihan and his wife Liz were never part of the glamorous Washington social scene. He didn't play golf. He didn't care much for the outdoors. He spent most of his time reading and writing.

He was always learning, always teaching. David Childs recounts a time when he was especially frustrated with some bureaucratic matter. Moynihan advised him that the government is filled with 90 percent bureaucrats, but it also has some of the most remarkable, talented individuals in every field. To be successful in government, he advised Childs, "You must seek out these extraordinary people and surround yourself with them." Moynihan did just that.

He sought out the best experts. He hired the most promising young people to join his staff, many of whom would advance to influential positions—people like Bob Peck, who would serve eventually as commissioner of the Public Buildings Service of the GSA, and Tim Russert, who would moderate "Meet the Press" and become Washington bureau chief of NBC News.

INDEPENDENT TO THE BONE

Another aspect of Moynihan's leadership was his role as a visionary and prophet. His colleague on the Senate Finance Committee, Bob Packwood, said Moynihan wasn't the conventional legislative craftsman; he was a "big-picture craftsman." [xxi] An editorial in the *Washington Post* describes him as "a man of large ideas in a city of tacticians, a visionary who nonetheless accomplished things." [xxii] Moynihan was practically alone in the Congress when he predicted the collapse of the Soviet Union in part due to ethnic conflict. He also understood before Ralph Nader spoke of it the link between the design of automobiles and safety, and wrote about it in his article, "Traffic Safety and the Body Politic." [xxiii]

Visionaries can be lonely, especially when one's prophecies are misunderstood, which happened to Moynihan with his 1965 report to President Johnson, "The Negro Family: The Case for National Action," now commonly known as the Moynihan Report. He discussed family structure as the key element. Drawing from the works of leading black sociologists of the day, Moynihan wrote that family instability, which was more prevalent among the poorer black population in post–World War II America than with white families, leads to higher proportions of black families on welfare. The data showed that the disparity was growing. Moynihan pointed out that the Negro family was crumbling and was impeding the black population's chances for advancing. But many black leaders, as well as many liberal activists, misunderstood and claimed Moynihan was a racist.

Although vindicated eventually, Moynihan was emotionally scarred by the experience. Bob Peck suggests that this critical, painful incident may have caused Moynihan to view himself as a kind of prophet. This would become his leadership role in the Senate: not only was he prescient about far-reaching political and socioeconomic changes, but he felt compelled to point out difficult truths that many other politicians would rather ignore.

PLANNING BEFORE SPENDING

When it was time to reauthorize the Federal Highway Act in 1990, Moynihan was the Senate proponent for the Intermodal Surface Transportation Efficiency Act, which passed in 1991. ISTEA leveled the playing field between highways and mass transit. People were stunned when Moynihan turned what everyone thought would be a routine highway bill reauthorization into a revolutionary approach to transportation funding by encouraging states to use federal funds for modes of transportation other than limited-access highways, and by calling for planning before spending.

Moynihan later recalled that he had been influenced by the findings of a study conducted in Florida that projected the number of interstate highways needed to connect Miami with Orlando by the year 2013. "The serious, straight-minded, I'm sure well-compensated engineering report came in at 22 lanes each way. I said, 'But what's left of Florida?'" Moynihan's ISTEA bill also allowed a percentage of highway funds to be used for "enhancements," meaning environmental and aesthetic improvements including creation of new wetlands, rehabilitation of historic transportation structures, and conversion of abandoned rail lines to bike trails.

> THE DEVELOPMENT OF ISTEA HAS TO BE VIEWED AS MOYNIHAN'S MOST COMPREHENSIVE DEMONSTRATION OF HIS COMMAND OF PUBLIC WORKS DATA, HIS CONCOMITANT RESISTANCE TO CONVENTIONAL OPINION, HIS UNDERSTANDING OF ECONOMICS AND POLITICS, AND HIS BELIEF THAT PUBLIC WORKS FUNDAMENTALLY DETERMINE DEVELOPMENT PATTERNS AND THE QUALITY OF LIFE. [XXIV]
>
> ROBERT PECK, FORMER CHIEF OF STAFF TO MOYNIHAN AND FORMER COMMISSIONER OF PUBLIC BUILDINGS SERVICE OF THE U.S. GENERAL SERVICES ADMINISTRATION

ARCHITECTURAL CONSCIENCE OF CONGRESS

Moynihan was fond of quoting Thomas Jefferson in that "design activity and political thought are indivisible." Both men viewed architecture as a physical manifestation of the American government. For Moynihan, public design is a public issue because it is a political fact. He equated good civic design with good government.

GOOD OR BAD ARCHITECTURE IS NOT AN OPTION. IT IS AS FUNDAMENTAL A SIGN OF THE COMPETENCE OF GOVERNMENT AS WILL BE FOUND. MEN WHO BUILD BAD BUILDINGS ARE BAD GOVERNORS. A PEOPLE THAT PERSISTS IN ELECTING SUCH MEN IS OPTING FOR BAD GOVERNMENT. DANIEL PATRICK MOYNIHAN, "ARCHITECTURE IN A TIME OF TROUBLE," 1967 ADDRESS TO THE HARVARD GRADUATE SCHOOL OF DESIGN NEW YORK ALUMNI DINNER

THE NOTION OF CIVITAS—THAT A PERSON HAS A RIGHT AND RESPONSIBILITY TO BE THERE AND PARTICIPATE IN THE PUBLIC SPACE—THAT'S WHAT IT MEANS TO BE A REPUBLIC. DANIEL PATRICK MOYNIHAN

Moynihan warned a group of architects in 1967, "If we are to save our cities and restore to American public life the sense of shared experience, trust, and common purpose that seems to be draining out of it, the quality of public design has got to be made a public issue because it is a political fact." He spoke of the need for a "public architecture of intimacy, one that brings people together in an experience of confidence and trust." [xxv]

Moynihan believed that it is our public design that forms our legacy. As with ancient Greece and Rome, we will be remembered for the buildings and cities we leave behind. He worried that in place of the great civic projects of yesterday—Lake Shore Drive in Chicago, or "the great parks and squares of San Francisco"—all we get today in many cities are "convention centers and hotels. Nothing to be remembered for." [xxvi]

At the ULI October 2001 annual meeting, held on the heels of the 9/11 tragedy, Moynihan told architecture critic Paul Goldberger that it was no accident that the terrorists attacked what is a symbol of high urbanization. "These acts won't change our civilization," he said, and the best defense against attacks on America's free society is to "concentrate, not scatter." Moynihan recognized that something special happens when people come together that doesn't happen when they are dispersed. "This is a moment not to be intimidated. The only way they [the terrorists] can win is if we change the way we live, and a lot of us live in cities."

Pat in his hat.

COURTESY MOYNIHAN FAMILY

Senator Moynihan believed that the heightened security measures in Washington following the 9/11 attacks were necessary in some instances, but not all. He worried that the increased presence of X-ray machines and armed guards was diminishing our enjoyment of shared civic spaces and eroding the public realm. This was the subject of his last article, "Principles of Liberty," in the *Washington Post,* published shortly before he died. [xxvii] Moynihan had frequently said that people shouldn't need a pass to enjoy the nation's main street. Pennsylvania Avenue would be a lively place, inviting to all people. Yet, just a few blocks away at his neighborhood library, which Moynihan noted was the only Mies building in the capital, patrons were wanded and watched by armed "library police." "The point of public space," said Moynihan, "is it should be open."

NOTES

i Robert Peck, "Daniel Patrick Moynihan and the Fall and Rise of Public Works," in Robert A. Katzmann, ed., *Daniel Patrick Moynihan: The Intellectual in Public Life* (Washington, D.C.: Woodrow Wilson Center Press; and Baltimore and London: Johns Hopkins University Press, 1998), pp. 68–96. The Festschrift summarizes papers presented at the celebration of the senator's 70th birthday. Peck's excellent essay is a comprehensive discussion of Moynihan's influence on public buildings, urban design, preservation, highways, and transit. Peck takes the view that Moynihan transformed the debate on public works and writes that Moynihan's "reinvention of a noble, humanist public architecture" was a 35-year quest starting with his authorship of the "Guiding Principles for Federal Architecture," and culminating with the rebirth of Pennsylvania Avenue.

ii U.S. General Services Administration, *Vision + Voice, Design Excellence in Federal Architecture: Building a Legacy* (Washington, D.C.: U.S. General Services Administration, 2003), p. 10. Under the direction of Marilyn Farley, the Office of Design Excellence and the Arts at GSA conducted oral histories in the summer and fall of 2002 with Moynihan and leading public officials, architects, and design professionals who discussed the 1962 "Guiding Principles," which became the rationale for a new approach to the design of government building and public spaces. Excerpts of the interviews were published in *Voice + Vision*. These interviews provided excellent historical background on the "Guiding Principles" and their legacy as well as helpful direction for the author's telephone interviews with some of the same individuals—Robert Peck and David Childs.

iii Daniel P. Moynihan, "Foreword," in Carol M. Highsmith and Ted Landphair, *Pennsylvania Avenue: America's Main Street* (Washington, D.C.: American Institute of Architects Press, 1988).

iv *Vision + Voice*, p. 10.

v U.S. House Committee on Public Works, "Report to the President by the Ad Hoc Committee on Federal Office Space, 87th Congress, 2nd session, 1 June 1962." Portions written by Moynihan include "Guiding Principles for Federal Architecture," 11–12, and "The Redevelopment of Pennsylvania Avenue," 12–15. The "Guiding Principles" set a new approach to the design of government buildings and public spaces.

vi Douglas Schoen, *Pat: a Biography of Daniel Patrick Moynihan* (New York: Harper & Row, 1967).

vii Author interview with David Childs; see also *Vision + Voice*, p. 16.

viii Moynihan, "Foreword," Highsmith and Landphair, *Pennsylvania Avenue*.

ix Recounted in Highsmith and Landphair, *Pennsylvania Avenue*.

x Ibid.

xi Robert Peck and William Walton, unpublished oral history of Daniel Patrick Moynihan, Washington, D.C., U.S. General Services Administration, September 25, 2002.

xii *Vision + Voice*, p. 14.

xiii Reed Kroloff, "GSA Must Still Work to Achieve Design Excellence," *Architecture*, January 2001.

xiv *Vision + Voice*, p. 10.

xv Unpublished correspondence between Moynihan and Frederick Papert, October 1991.

xvi Daniel P. Moynihan, "The Politics of Conservancy" (Lecture to the New York Landmarks Conservancy at the Metropolitan Museum of Art, New York, November 7, 1984).

xvii Moynihan, "Foreword," Highsmith and Landphair, *Pennsylvania Avenue*.

xviii Moynihan, "Politics of Conservancy." See also Daniel Patrick Moynihan for Robert Peck's discussion of Moynihan's "critical faculty in architecture," pp 89–90.

xix *Vision + Voice*, p. 19.

xx Moynihan, "Politics of Conservancy."

xxi Katzmann, ed., *Daniel Patrick Moynihan*, p. 77.

xxii "Editorial," *Washington Post,* March 27, 2003.

xxiii Daniel P. Moynihan, *Coping: Essays in the Practice of Government* (New York: Random House, 1973) pp. 79–99.

xxiv Katzmann, ed., *Daniel Patrick Moynihan*, p. 77.

xxv Daniel P. Moynihan, "Architecture in a Time of Trouble," *AIA Journal,* September 1969.

xxvi Moynihan, "Foreword," Highsmith and Landphair, *Pennsylvania Avenue*.

xxvii Daniel P. Moynihan, "Principles of Liberty," *Washington Post,* February 3, 2003.

PRIMARY REFERENCES

Highsmith, Carol M., and Ted Landphair. *Pennsylvania Avenue: America's Main Street.* Washington, D.C.: American Institute of Architects Press, 1988.

Hodgson, Godfrey. *The Gentleman from New York: Daniel Patrick Moynihan.* Boston: Houghton Mifflin Company, 2000.

Katzmann, Robert A., ed. *Daniel Patrick Moynihan: The Intellectual in Public Life.* Washington, D.C.: Woodrow Wilson Center Press; and Baltimore and London: Johns Hopkins University Press, 1998.

Moynihan, Daniel P. "Architecture in a Time of Trouble." *AIA Journal,* September 1969.

Moynihan, Daniel P. "New Roads and Urban Chaos." *The Reporter,* April 14, 1960.

Moynihan, Daniel P. "The Politics of Conservancy." (Lecture to the New York Landmarks Conservancy at the Metropolitan Museum of Art, New York, November 7, 1984.)

Moynihan, Elizabeth. (E-mail correspondence with author, March and April 2004).

Schoen, Douglas. *Pat: A Biography of Daniel Patrick Moynihan.* New York: Harper & Row, 1967.

U.S. General Services Administration. *Vision + Voice, Design Excellence in Federal Architecture: Building a Legacy.* Washington, D.C.: U.S. General Services Administration, 2003.

AUTHOR INTERVIEWS

Kent Barwick, president, Municipal Art Society, March 2004, by telephone.

M. Jay Brodie, president, Baltimore Development Corporation, March 2004, by telephone.

David M. Childs, FAIA, design consulting partner at New York office of Skidmore, Owings & Merrill, March 2004, by telephone.

Jo-Ann Neuhaus, executive director, Pennsylvania Quarter Neighborhood Association, February 2004.

Frederick Papert, president, 42nd Street Development Corporation, March 2004, by telephone.

Robert Peck, president, Greater Washington Board of Trade, March 2004, by telephone.

Alexandros Washburn, AIA, partner at New York office of W Architecture, March 2004, by telephone.

John Woodbridge, first executive director, Pennsylvania Avenue Development Corporation, March 2004, by telephone.

OTHER SOURCES

Blumenthal, Sidney. "To the Pennsylvania Station." *New Yorker*, March 14, 1994.

Dean, Andrea Oppenheimer. "Moynihan Beams as Polshek Unveils Newseum Design for D.C." *Architectural Record*, 2002.

Forgey, Benjamin. "The Senator Who Paved the Way: Pat Moynihan Helped Shape America's Main Street." *Washington Post*, March 27, 2003.

Gill, Brendan. "McKim's Monuments." *New Yorker*, March 14, 1994.

Goldberger, Paul. Discussion with Moynihan at ULI fall meeting in Boston, October 2001.

Kroloff, Reed. "GSA Must Still Work to Achieve Design Excellence." *Architecture*, January 2001.

Moynihan, Daniel P., and Frederick Papert. Unpublished correspondence, October 1991.

Takesuye, David. "America's Main Street." *Urban Land*, October 2001, pp. 34–39.

HE HAS A SPECIAL FEEL FOR WHAT HE WANTS.
HE LOOKS FOR A POINT OF DIFFERENCE THAT
WILL STAND OUT. | PHILIP JOHNSON
ARCHITECT

GERALD D. HINES

DEVELOPER EXTRAORDINAIRE

WHAT ENERGIZES GERALD HINES? Surely, his prime motivator is the opportunity to create great buildings in markets that value architectural distinction. Hines constantly reaffirms his goal of luring the top of the market by commissioning the highest-quality architecture for his projects. But there is more to Hines than an appreciation for architectural excellence. He says it himself: he really enjoys building. He is energized by the excitement of constructing outstanding buildings, of taking on complex projects that present new challenges.

His colleagues, chosen for their entrepreneurial spirit, also talk about Hines's quest for certainty in how a building's design will work—to satisfy future tenants' space and service needs, to maintain operational reliability, to overcome intricate structural and mechanical hurdles, and finally to obtain the best space for the money. They mention the way Hines probes each facet of a development, defining potential problems and seeking innovative solutions. They also talk about the strength of the collaborative corporate structure Hines invented as business expanded beyond Houston and then beyond the United States. And there is no doubt who made that happen: the man whose name is on the letterhead.

DAD IS A UNIQUE INDIVIDUAL, A REALLY ENERGETIC GUY.
JEFFREY HINES

HOUSTON, WE HAVE LIFTOFF

Gerald Hines is one of the best-known real estate developers in the business. He has created hundreds of buildings, many of them award-winning architectural triumphs. The Hines organization has become a full-service real estate firm engaged in building development, investment, and management across the United States and throughout the world. His company has grown to 2,900

Gerald Hines at topping out celebration for Post Oak Tower in the Galleria. Architect: Philip Johnson.

The Galleria in Houston, now a 3 million-square-foot mixed-use complex, won the first ULI Award for Excellence in 1979. Architect: Hellmuth, Obata & Kassabaum.

employees. All this from a standing start in 1952 as a fledgling developer doing small office buildings and warehouses in Houston. Energetic, indeed.

Gerald Hines was born in Gary, Indiana, in 1925. His father was superintendent of electrical systems for U.S. Steel, the main source of jobs in Gary. During the early years of World War II, when U.S. Steel was looking for laborers anywhere they could find them, young Hines, then in high school, spent weekends as part of the "labor gang." The mind-numbing heat, dirt, and physical exertion of that experience, he says, gave him plenty of motivation to pursue higher education and a more interesting career. The Army intervened after high school, however, and he spent the remainder of the war as a lieutenant in the combat engineers. Hines was about to be shipped to Japan when the war ended.

He came back to Indiana to obtain a degree in mechanical engineering from Purdue University in 1948. When he had a choice of locations for his first job he picked Houston, which, as the home of several fraternity brothers, would provide a friendly start to his working life. At the time, Houston was enjoying an economic boom—fueled by the oil business—which opened up many career opportunities. Much of his job as an engineering consultant focused on designing mechanical systems for the new commercial buildings popping up everywhere. Says Hines, "I just got to know buildings very well. Then I thought I would like to build them."[ii]

His first opportunity at development came in 1952 when a neighbor expressed a need for a new building. Hines said he could build it, and did—a relatively straightforward combination of office and warehouse space. With development opportunities flowering throughout the Houston area, Hines developed several more office/warehouse buildings and finally set up shop as a full-fledged developer in 1957 in southwest Houston.

By the tenth anniversary of his firm, then known as Gerald D. Hines Interests, Hines had completed 97 office, warehouse, retail, parking, and residential projects. It was one of the largest development organizations in Houston, with a staff of 35 employees. In the next two years, the firm moved decisively into office development along the West Loop (Interstate 610) and opened the 22-story Post Oak Tower in 1970, the first entry in a series of office towers in that location.

Hines's first home run in developing distinctive, "watch this!" projects came in 1970 with the opening of the first phase of the Houston Galleria in the Post Oak area. Hines commissioned Hellmuth, Obata & Kassabaum to design the 33-acre project. An enclosed shopping center of 420,000 square feet plus an adjoining Neiman Marcus store, it took as a model Milan's 19th-century Galleria Vittorio Emanuele, famous for its elegant glass-covered arcade of high-end shops and restaurants. The Houston Galleria's spectacular barrel-vaulted skylights now surmount 2.5 million square feet of space for more than 375 stores and restaurants and a splendid ice rink for recreational skating. Including a 2003 expansion after its sale to Simon Property Group, the mall is the fifth largest in the United States. Neiman Marcus, Saks Fifth Avenue, and Nordstrom are there, as are Tiffany & Co., Cartier, and Gucci. But the shopping mall is only part of the complex, which developed in phases over 27 years. It also includes two hotels and three office towers. (The startlingly slender Williams Tower is just across the street.)

One Shell Plaza, completed in 1971, was Hines's first high-rise project in downtown Houston. Architect: Skidmore, Owings & Merrill.

Hines followed up the Galleria opening with another clear-the-bases building, One Shell Plaza, his first high-rise project in downtown Houston. He brought in Bruce Graham of Skidmore, Owings & Merrill, considered the corporate architecture firm *par excellence,* to design the building. Fifty stories high, at its opening in 1971 it was the tallest building west of the Mississippi River. It also was the highest reinforced concrete structure in the world, built to withstand hurricane winds. The building is clad in Italian travertine marble; wind-bracing columns at eight points give the impression of an undulating facade. According to Hines, the building originally was conceived as the regional office of the Shell Oil Company, but once head office personnel laid eyes on the architectural drawings, it was commandeered for Shell's world headquarters. The regional office was constructed over the adjoining parking structure. A shopping mall beneath the building connects to Houston's network of subsurface tunnels.

Hines was concerned about the project's cost from the beginning. Using reinforced concrete for the structure helped to reduce construction costs, but Hines was also interested in lowering the cost of interior renovations, because he recognized that Shell would be turning over about a third of the

floor space each year. He directed the architects to raise the ceiling height from the standard 11 feet to 13 feet, 4 inches, to gain space to handle low-pressure ductwork. More expensive at the time, it proved a cost-saving feature over the long term. It also helped reduce the unforeseen cost of asbestos removal years later.[iii] Hines also built the 25-story Two Shell Plaza in 1972 next to One Shell Plaza to absorb the overflow needs of the Shell Oil Company. Today, Hines retains an ownership interest in One and Two Shell Plaza and management responsibilities for both towers.

With these two projects, Hines signaled his admiration for top-quality architectural design, his intent to target the high end of the market, and his willingness to pursue innovative structural and other cost-saving methods. While making his mark on the Houston skyline, he established his trademark approach to real estate development, one that achieved liftoff for a national and then an international practice.

Hines with a model of One Shell Plaza. Architect: Skidmore, Owings & Merrill.

RESPECT FOR ARCHITECTS

Gerald Hines's education in mechanical engineering would not ordinarily foretell an interest in architectural design. Hines himself is uncertain about just how he came to admire the work of architects. His younger days in the steel town of Gary, Indiana, certainly did nothing to awaken an interest in building design. Even his family's frequent visits to Chicago's premier collection of fine architecture failed to ignite any particular passion in him for the design of buildings. His Purdue education included no courses related to architecture. When Hines moved to Houston, the city was just coming to life as a metropolis, with few interesting buildings to excite interest in architecture.

Yet, his designs for building systems—heating, air conditioning, utilities, and the like—required attention to the exterior and interior performance qualities of structures and materials. It is not much of a stretch to go from that concern to an interest in the architectural features of a building. Moreover, Hines's budding interest in developing buildings awakened his respect for the potential marketing advantage of a building's appearance. His early ventures were building

BUILDINGS OF QUALITY, BACKED BY RESPONSIVE, PROFESSIONAL MANAGEMENT, ATTRACT BETTER TENANTS, COMMAND HIGHER RENTS, AND RETAIN THEIR VALUE DESPITE THE UPS AND DOWNS OF THE REAL ESTATE MARKET. GERALD HINES

combination office/warehouses, structures whose typical appearance was rather mundane—single-story, inexpensively produced, boxlike buildings surrounded by parking, and usually located in back-lot parts of town. Hines believed that design improvements might give him a competitive edge, and employed the dean of the University of Texas architecture school to do some creative thinking about design ideas. His next building made an impact in the marketplace with some rather modest but visible design changes: brick instead of clay tile facades, a handsome stone ledge, a nicely shaped canopy. None cost a great deal more than the usual materials but signaled "quality" in a market of generally humdrum structures.

From this experience he learned two valuable lessons: 1) Good design need not add substantial costs, and 2) Good design attracts market interest. "A well-designed building," he says, "is the first to fill up—the main objective, after all—and the last to get vacated."

With the Galleria and the One Shell Plaza buildings, Hines took his first step into the world of big-name architects, the trendsetters of architectural design in the United States and the world. He has collaborated since then with such well-known architects as I.M. Pei, Frank Gehry, Philip Johnson, Cesar Pelli, and Robert A. M. Stern, as well as distinguished designers in the metropolitan regions in which he has developed buildings. He has become known in architectural circles as a patron of good design, a modern Medici who is willing to underwrite extraordinary conceptions of building design, always understanding the financial advantages of prestigious buildings. Although architects, like many in the creative professions, can become prima donnas (Vincent Scully calls them "hero-architects"), Hines says he has had only one experience with a "difficult" designer, and "that architect hasn't worked for me again."

Hines comments that architects need a knowledgeable client who understands what makes sense for the site and marketplace; successful architects appreciate that skill. "There's a right architect for every site," he says, "and when we sometimes ask several designers for ideas [about a proposed project], something will hit us between the eyes—that's the guy for this project." Louis Sklar, an executive vice president with Hines, explained that the organization chooses architects based on their compatibility with clients, especially high-profile clients. Philip Johnson credits Hines with introducing him to clients with whom he worked easily and who commissioned him for other work.[iv]

Hines became known as a collaborator with well-known architects. One of his favorites, Philip Johnson, is pictured here.

Hines's reputation as a patron of finely crafted buildings gained national prominence by his development of Pennzoil Place in 1975. To design the corporate headquarters of the Pennzoil Company

Pennzoil Place was dubbed the Building of the Decade in 1975 by *New York Times* architecture critic Ada Louise Huxtable due to its dramatic sculptural silhouette. Architect: Burgee/Johnson Architects.

in Houston, Hines brought in the renowned architect Philip Johnson, of the Johnson and Burgee office in New York. Johnson turned out a creative design that set new standards for high-rise office buildings. One admirer comments that Pennzoil Place was "one of the most architecturally influential buildings constructed in the United States during the 1970s and 1980s. Its combination of unusual design, high style, and shrewd entrepreneurship made [it] a model for the generation of tall office buildings designed during the last quarter of the 20th century."[v] Ada Louise Huxtable, then the architecture critic for the *New York Times*, called it a "towering achievement," and the design was influential in Philip Johnson's receiving the Gold Medal of the American Institute of Architects in 1978 and winning the Pritzker Prize in Architecture in 1979.

Pennzoil Place consists of two sleek towers, 36 stories high, joined by a space-frame lobby that rises eight stories at its juncture with the towers. The trapezoidal, glass-faced towers, only ten feet apart, contain 1.8 million square feet of space. In the Houston tradition, a basement floor connects to the system of underground shopping arcades and to a 550-car parking garage.

The Pennzoil Place design responded to several conditions that reveal the complexities of decisions demanded of the design. J. Hugh Liedtke, chairman of the Pennzoil Company, told Johnson that he wanted, in Johnson's words, "a building with character that would stand out from the undecorated glass boxes around town."[vi] Liedtke thought an unusual top to the building would help, and also asked for plenty of natural light. As the developer, Hines wanted the building to have a distinct identity for more than one major tenant. Johnson responded by designing two buildings, shaped as trapezoids with corners almost touching—a laborious trial-and-error design process. They also had glass roofs tilted at a 45-degree angle, "for fun, just to do something like that," Johnson comments. Liedtke liked the design because it was different from that of any other building in Houston, but Hines wanted to compare the cost of the slanted top with that of a flat-topped design. According to Johnson, Liedtke immediately disliked the model of the flat-topped version. At that point, Johnson pulled off the fan-shaped lobby element and placed it on top of the building, demonstrating the effect of a slanted roof. Liedtke okayed it at once. When the buildings were completed, with the slanted tops, Hines discovered that unusual space under the roofs would rent at much higher prices than the rest of the building—today, in fact, tenants who want that upper space are required to rent space in the lower floors as well. Johnson also discovered that this break away from what he called "Miesian clarity" (referring to the doyen of modern architecture, Mies van der Rohe) was the shape of the future—what he called his "historical period."

Architecture critic Paul Heyer calls Pennzoil Place "geographically manipulative. . . . Here a simple geometric idea . . . affords total visual clarity to the design." The twin towers are mirror images of each other, Heyer observes, and the narrow vertical slot between the buildings makes them a changing visual presence in the urban landscape.[vii] Another critic, Vincent Scully, although skeptical of the pedestrian eye view of the buildings, considered Pennzoil Place a beguiling sculptural presence on the Houston skyline.

Philip Johnson went on to design several more projects for the Hines organization, including the Transco Tower (now Williams Tower) and RepublicBank Center (now Bank of America Center), both in Houston, and United Bank Center (now Wells Fargo Center) in Denver. Hines quickly sold Pennzoil Place to the Deutsche Bank of Germany, and in 1999 a German-led group of European investors acquired the project. Originally developed for about $50 million, it sold for over $200 million.

THE LARGER CONTEXT

Though Hines is known for his signature towers that make a distinctive imprint on city skylines, he prefers to create clusters of buildings that "make a place." Well-planned multistructure projects, he says, can include a mix of uses that complement each other and add up to more than the sum of their parts. "It's not just retail and office space—you must also have other elements such as housing and recreation that interact to create a high-quality collection of buildings."

Hines's development in the Post Oak area of Houston early in his career exemplifies his interest in making an impact through clustering a series of building projects. The Post Oak Central was the

Completed in November 2001, Diagonal Mar Centre is the largest shopping and leisure center in Catalonia, Spain. Architect: Robert A.M. Stern.

first of many office complexes Hines developed in the area, including three buildings clustered around a lake, the Transco Tower complex, and the Houston Galleria complex—a variety of projects that creates a distinctive urban center. Hines also developed the First Colony planned community on 9,700 acres in Sugar Land near Houston. A long-term project initiated in 1973 and completed in 1999, the community encompasses 15,000 homes, a regional shopping mall, industrial and office development, churches, schools, and municipal services.

Hines frequently develops suburban office parks such as the Cedar Court complex in the Seattle area, consisting of four buildings totaling 430,000 square feet of office space. Completed in 1999 and occupied by Microsoft, it was sold to the tenant in 2002. A more complicated multistructure project was Hines's renovation of the Renaissance Center in Detroit, the global headquarters of General Motors. In 2000, Hines's client expanded the project to include a 25-acre mixed-use development and urban park called River East.

Hines is especially proud of the Diagonal Mar development in Barcelona, Spain. Located on 84 acres next to the Mediterranean Sea, it is a $600 million mixed-use community that was planned to include 1,400 apartments, a regional retail and leisure center, three hotels, three office buildings, and a 540,000-square-foot convention facility. A 35-acre public park surrounds it and opens the project up to the waterfront. In 2004, most of the project has been completed. All of the infrastructure and the park have been open to the public for two years. The retail center and two of the three hotels are open. Three of the five residential phases are finished and the fourth is under construction. The three office buildings have just been completed. And next to the project, on land donated by Hines, the city government has put up an office building, a new hotel, and the largest convention center in Spain. A considerable achievement for a project in deep trouble before Hines acquired it in 1996, it stands as an example of Hines's identifying an opportunity and seizing a strategic acquisition.

As a Houstonian now living part-time in London, Hines deplores the long-term trend in the United States of almost total dependence on the automobile, requiring time-consuming commutes within haphazardly developed, poorly connected urban areas. His experience with the tightly linked, pedestrian-friendly development common in European cities gives him hope that more Americans will choose denser living spaces with transit opportunities, and that more developers will create them. "We will develop denser cores," he says, "because people will demand them. They'll pay a higher price per square foot to increase their discretionary time."

Reflecting on Hines's intellectual shift, Joseph E. Brown, president of the EDAW, Inc., planning and design firm and member of the ULI jury that selected Hines as the 2002 winner of the J.C. Nichols prize, comments: "Gerry Hines has moved beyond signature buildings to a level of concern with infrastructure, parks, and the public realm. . . . It's a remarkable evolution from the best architecture to the best overall design to the best community. Gerry builds communities with a sense that they will be here forever."

WORKING STYLE

Hines is a detail man. Engineers tend to be that way and Hines is no exception to the archetype. His associates expect and prepare for sharp questions about every aspect of proposed projects, from the building's solar orientation to the ceiling height and the type of energy monitoring system to be used. Yet, they

THE PENNZOIL BUILDING IS A COOL BUILDING. I WORKED THERE FOR FIVE YEARS ON THE 31ST FLOOR. I HAD AN OFFICE ON THE SIDE WHERE THE FLOOR-TO-CEILING GLASS WALL SLOPES IN. IT WAS A VERY AWESOME OFFICE. AND WAS SO COOL WHEN IT RAINED AND THE WATER POURED DOWN THE SIDES! BETT, ONLINE MESSAGE, WWW.HOUSTONARCHITECTURE.INFO

also know well his overriding interest in producing great buildings and distinctive projects. They have heard him say, repeatedly, "For us, there is never a choice between building the mediocre or the magnificent. People expect high quality from us and providing it has paid off." Hines's working mode combines the unbeatable attributes of establishing a well-defined goal and intensely pursuing ways to achieve that goal. Gerald Hines's commitment to being the best while remaining fiscally responsible has created a brand of excellence for his company: the Hines name has become synonymous with quality—of architecture, building materials and systems, sustainability, and business operations.

Fellow developer Peter Rummell observes, "Gerry has a detailed view of the world as well as a global view, and good design comes from paying a lot of attention to details. You have to start with a vision . . . but then you have to execute that vision, and the execution is in the details. That's not something you phone in. It's something you spend a lot of hours poring over. You put yourself in the consumer's position of how that project will be experienced. Some people don't know how to do this. Gerry does."

Hines's man in London, Michael Topham, executive vice president of Hines's European operation, explains his boss's attitude this way: "He has a genuine quest for understanding what he's looking at or pursuing, whether it's engineering design or the carbohydrates in food products. He uses the word 'why' and the phrase 'I don't understand' constantly to obtain more information about matters he's interested in. He regards every project as a challenge to build a better product. And at the same time, he's a most thoroughly nice guy."

Philip Johnson cites an example of Hines's penchant for detail in the design of the elevator systems for the Transco Tower. The secret for achieving the building's needle-like slenderness, he said, "was one of Gerry's brilliant ideas." Ordinarily, the designer would have provided separate elevator shafts for low, middle, and high stories, taking up lots of space. But putting the high-rise shaft on top of the low-rise one, with an elevator exchange point midway, saved space and cost, and produced additional rentable square footage. For Gerald Hines, says Johnson, "it was cost figuring. For us architects . . . it made a tall, thin needle instead of a clunky building."[viii]

Developing Diagonal Mar in Spain was challenging on several fronts, including taking over the project from a previous developer and working through the complex approval process typical of European countries. Hines decided to become personally involved in bringing this project to fruition, sorting out the economic and design issues as well as the regulatory obstacles. Hines says that working within foreign regulatory regimes is no more daunting than developing buildings in San Francisco or Boston, two places he claims are tough on developers. Hines credits Barcelona's planning and design official assigned to the Diagonal Mar project with contributing several good ideas, including opening up the proposed urban park all the way to the sea by imaginative siting of high-rise buildings.

One example of the project's complications was the major investment required to prevent water filtration into the underground garage along the waterfront. To accomplish this, Hines had to build a half-mile-long wall 200 feet below grade. The wall proved problematic when it was discovered that the design for tiebacks to hold the wall in place had been miscalculated. The delay for redesign and reconstruction added nine months to the construction process. The project architect, Robert A.M. Stern, commented that the entire project required a complicated design, but "it is Mr. Hines's nature to roll up his sleeves and find solutions to obstacles. He doesn't shy away from tackling complex, controversial projects."

HINES AS INNOVATOR

Finding solutions often takes Hines into the guts of the building design, the mechanical, electrical, and other operating systems that make the building habitable, subjects familiar to him since predeveloper days. He has no compunction about sitting down with the engineers to pore over the drawings and discuss the equipment options. Perhaps that is the genesis of his interest in environmentally conscious "green" buildings. For years, Hines has sought progressively to improve energy efficiency in his buildings, including sophisticated energy monitoring systems, and energy-saving windows, ventilation systems, and other fixtures and equipment.

The company developed and is implementing a proprietary energy management software program called Hines Utility Monitoring and Management Tool (HUMMT). The program allows accurate recording and analysis of energy and utility use in buildings. The company also has formulated and employed a water treatment standard, a chiller efficiency monitoring and testing standard, a refrigerant management program, and indoor air quality guidelines. In addition, Hines adopted innovative systems such as outside air economizers, mold-resistant shaft liners, and underfloor air distribution systems. Kenneth Hubbard, executive vice president of Hines's east region, says, "I think people at Hines are willing to push hard on product innovation and we really believe that's where we get our competitive advantage." [ix]

Since 1992, the company has been a partner in the U.S. Environmental Protection Agency's ENERGY STAR program, which recognizes projects meeting EPA standards for superior energy management and conservation. Hines's projects have received 74 ENERGY STAR Label awards as of 2004, and the company was named ENERGY STAR Partner of the year for three years running. In 2004, the EPA recognized Hines with the ENERGY STAR Sustained Excellence Award for its continued leadership in superior energy management. Hines also has five projects listed in the U.S. Green Building Council's pilot program of LEED for Existing Buildings. [x]

Eugene Kohn of Kohn Pedersen Fox believes that Hines's willingness to take risks and try innovative approaches encourages architects and project managers to be more daring. "Gerry does not surround himself with 'yes' people," he notes. "He wants other opinions, he listens to his team and his architects, and is always ready to learn something new."

DEVELOPING THE CORPORATE STRUCTURE

One of the development industry's firmest principles is that development is best done by local firms that can closely track the regional market and understand the ins and outs of local regulatory processes. An allied principle is that American developers had best stick to developing in the United States, given the regulatory and other constraints they expect to confront in foreign nations. Hines has violated both principles—or overcome them by grit and hard work. He has done so by evolving a corporate structure that emphasizes local decision-making responsibilities, augmented by regional and centralized expertise and financial

The company is headed by Gerald Hines as chairman and his son Jeffrey Hines, pictured here, as president.

resources. As of 2004, Hines has five regional offices that express the company's international reach: Western United States and Asia Pacific (San Francisco); Eastern United States (New York); Southwestern United States, also responsible for Eurasia and Mexico (Houston); Midwestern United States and South America (Chicago); Southeastern United States (Atlanta); and Europe/Middle East (London). Hines also has offices in 36 metropolitan areas and 69 cities in the United States and in 12 foreign countries. Hines's one-man enterprise working out of a small office in Houston has matured into a powerhouse organization with 2,900 employees. In 2004, 49 projects are under construction. The privately owned firm's portfolio of projects that are completed, underway, or managed consists of more than 700 properties. It is one of the largest real estate organizations in the world and controls assets valued at approximately $14 billion.

From the top down, the company is headed by Gerald Hines as chairman and Jeffrey Hines, his son, as president. The Hines executive committee also includes the partners who head the five regional offices outside Houston and two senior financial partners. All have 30 or more years of service within the organization—a strong expression of company loyalty and, perhaps more important, of long-term accumulation of expertise in development.

But Hines is a great believer in bottom-up management, in assigning responsibility to local project managers for planning and completing projects on budget and programmed for the most profitable market. Hines initially structured his development organization like many others, by enlarging his Houston office as his activities expanded. However, as he took on more projects outside Houston, Hines recognized that real estate inherently is a local business and determined that the company could best grow through a decentralized organization that relied on local management talent. Michael Topham underscores the importance of local project managers: "The energy and vision of local people wherever they may be are the key to Hines's success."

But Hines also wanted to make available to local project managers the expertise that resides in the senior members of the organization, particularly in view of the variety of projects the firm was engaging in. To accomplish this, Hines created what might be called "augmented decentralization." Regional offices managed by senior members of the firm were created to establish a permanent presence in key hub markets and to develop local staffs. While key decisions are made at the regional level, both Gerald and Jeffrey Hines visit projects of special interest to offer their advice, and other staff with expertise in particular aspects of development are made available for consultation. For all but the smallest projects, these forces are brought together in a project team, with roving specialists brought in from time to time as needed. Best of all, the organizational model can be expanded as the need arises.

Hines added a significant feature to this team-formation scenario: with responsibility comes financial participation in the project. In contrast with most publicly traded companies, however, participation does not come in the form of stock options, independent of the specific product. Instead, staff involved in the project team are allocated a financial share in the project, whether the project is built to sell or built to hold. Thus, they have an incentive to plan and deliver the best project for the site, client, and market. Moreover, they retain a financial interest in the project until it passes out of Hines's portfolio.

> WHEN WE OPEN AN OFFICE, WE BRING IN PEOPLE WHO HAVE GROWN UP WITHIN HINES, WHO KNOW THE CULTURE AND KNOW HOW WE OPERATE. WE ALSO BRING IN PEOPLE FROM THE LOCAL MARKETS WHO KNOW THE VAGARIES OF THE AREA. [XI]
>
> JEFFREY HINES

Robert Hollister, vice president at Hines's Seattle office, describes how this process works for him. The essence of the young, upwardly mobile manager, Hollister came to Hines after five years in a variety of jobs (school teacher, Microsoft software engineer) and a return to college for a graduate degree in business management. Liking the idea of creating tangible products, he joined the Hines San Francisco office in 1996, then a year and a half later moved to head the new Seattle office. As local manager, he is responsible for creating business for the firm in the Seattle area, generating project ideas, and making judgments in planning, design, construction, and property management. During six years on the job, he has overseen three projects through completion, including the 40-story IDX Tower at Fourth and Madison and two suburban office clusters, and is now finishing the design phase of a build-to-suit medical office building for Evergreen Hospital.

Hollister ticks off three important ways that the company's depth of expertise supports his efforts. One is the role of the regional partner as a mentor for local managers. His regional manager helps him identify and evaluate project opportunities, offers advice as potential projects are packaged, suggests involvement of specialists both inside and outside the organization, assists with formation of project teams, and periodically checks project progress. At every step, questions are asked and proposals are examined to reach decisions at important phases in the development process. In some organizations, this process might bog down in bureaucratic paper shuffling or stifle initiative,

but both Hollister and Topham say the high level of interaction throughout the firm functions as a system of checks and balances for sound decision making.

For Hollister, the financial resources made available by the company are extremely important. Hines has attracted a host of investors, such as institutions and pension funds, who are confident of the firm's capabilities to hatch profitable projects. In addition, Hines has been forming funds as financial vehicles for investments in certain types of development. Thus, the Hines organization often has a ready source of capital when a local manager seeks financial support for a new project. Hollister says that two of his projects have tapped $180 million from such funds. Not only are funds available in the amounts and quality required for the project, but the availability of funding relieves the local project manager of the time required to ferret out financial sources.

Completed in 1983, the 64-story, 1.6 million-square-foot Williams Tower is located adjacent to the Galleria mixed-use center. Architect: Philip Johnson and John Burgee.

The third strength of the organizational structure is the centralized expertise it makes available to local managers. Given the wide array of product types, construction methods, planning issues, and design options in today's development practice, local managers can use all the help they can get for all but the most mundane projects. Depending on the issues presented by a specific project, staff from other offices, regions, or the central office are frequently brought in for consultation with local managers. Hines's central office has established four groups that can assist development managers: corporate finance, corporate communications, operations and engineering services, and one named "conceptual construction," which focuses on innovative construction methods. Hollister, never having developed a 40-story office building before, benefited from the availability of this kind of in-house expertise to assist in the formulation of his development strategy.

Developing abroad tested the capabilities of the organization to wade into new markets and new ways of development. Hines's approach was to establish a solid base of experienced employees for offices in foreign nations, then add local expertise.

Americans must spend time in a new market to gain credibility, and local talent often needs to broaden its knowledge to compete internationally. Combining the value of real estate know-how with a local perspective, according to Jeff Hines, "gives us the best of both worlds." Hines also has partnered with locally based, well-connected organizations. Hines associated with UPDK in Russia—the agency with the exclusive right under the former communist system to develop for non-Soviet entities, and the owner of substantial property interests retained after the dissolution of the Soviet Union. And in Mexico, Hines has developed a series of projects with the Metropolis group of wealthy Mexican families.[xii]

The "augmented decentralization" model, with its strong support for local managers and financial participation in project development, underscores the value that the Hines organization places on its employees. Hines's corporate culture values the entrepreneurial spirit that has always activated developers, but also encourages new ways of thinking by challenging professionals to develop strategies tailored to each building and its future occupants. Employees are given opportunities to make educated decisions and set in motion innovative solutions to development issues. Hubbard says, "The people who choose to work at Hines—they're curious, they're looking for challenges, and they're looking to create things in which they can take enormous pride."[xiii]

The 64-foot waterwall is one of several special features of the Williams Tower. Architect: Philip Johnson and John Burgee.

BUILDING FINANCIAL RESOURCES

Hines has a history of financing new buildings with a high level of equity rather than the strong proportion of debt financing sought by many developers. It was not always so. He borrowed to finance his first projects and put his profits into the next building. But he reconsidered that strategy after risking his entire net worth, about $5 million, to develop the Houston Galleria and the 50-story One Shell Plaza at the same time. Hines said later, "That was crazy; I said I'd never do that again."[xiv] Rather than borrow, Hines found equity investors such as European pension funds and the investment office of Kuwait. Typically, Hines invests 5 to 15 percent of the equity in each project, and in addition receives a percentage of any profits generated from the sale.

In the 1990s, the firm attracted a group of investors that provided funding for many projects, and increasingly the company is establishing funds as financing vehicles. Its first venture was to establish the Emerging Markets Fund with Dean Witter and the Trust Company of the West Group in 1995. Capitalized with $410 million, mostly from the U.S. pension funds, the fund focused on development opportunities in formerly communist countries, plus other emerging markets. When that fund closed with 80 percent of the funds committed, Hines formed a second emerging markets fund, this one focused in large part on Russia and Asia. This was followed by the Hines U.S. Office Development Fund and Hines Corporate Properties LLC, which invest primarily in construction of suburban office projects. The U.S. Office Development Fund is backed by three institutional investors, and Hines Corporate Properties was created in partnership with a major institutional investor. As of 2004, Hines has established ten such funds.

This strategy of establishing funds as financing vehicles has been so successful in attracting investors and making capital available for development that Jeff Hines says the company expects to form one or two such funds every year, each with a distinct investment focus such as single-tenant buildings or European development. The payoff is that Hines's development opportunities are not constrained by its access to capital. Jeff Hines says, "In the old days, we'd find the opportunity and then find the capital. Today, in many cases, we have the capital all arranged and we go out and find the opportunity." [xv] Jeff Hines adds: "It is more persuasive to go to a landowner or the owner of a building and say 'we can write a check' than to say 'let's sign a letter of intent and we'll go and try to find capital.'" [xvi] In addition, the emphasis on equity financing allows Hines more latitude in adjusting rents to reflect market cycles. Kenneth Hubbard sums up the advantages for Hines: "This puts us in a position to have capital that can act in a discretionary manner and to be more responsive to where the development opportunities are." [xvii]

WE ARE A MUCH MORE BROADLY BASED FIRM TODAY, AND OUR GOAL IS TO BE ACTIVE IN ALL PHASES OF THE [REAL ESTATE] CYCLE.

JEFFREY HINES

Another approach to financing came through Hines's development experience with the banking and financial community. Since the 1970s, Hines has focused on developing headquarters buildings for the financial sector. According to Hubbard, this approach evolved as Hines built more and more buildings for banks and real estate finance institutions, and eventually was developing larger buildings in joint ventures with commercial banks. As we worked with a bank, says Hubbard, "we learned all we could about the functional objectives of the bank and responded with our expertise and deal structures," eventually forming partnerships with banks to carry out the projects. "Since then, we have established relationships with a lot of the major financial firms and have done some of the most sophisticated, technologically oriented headquarters imaginable." [xviii] For example, in what Cushman & Wakefield's Bruce Mosler called "a difficult market to crack," Hines has developed office towers in

New York City for Bear Stearns, Morgan Stanley Dean Witter, and Goldman Sachs.[xix]

Of course, none of this would be possible without the Hines brand on its products. Like all good businesses, financial firms like to be on the winner's side. They understand and value the solid performance and long-lasting value of Hines's roster of development projects.

MORE THAN A DEVELOPMENT COMPANY

Michael Topham describes today's Hines organization as a full-service real estate company providing four areas of business expertise beyond that of project development:

□ Acquisition for investments of buildings developed by others;

□ Development management for other owners—similar to the design/build concept;

□ Property management of both Hines-owned and other owners' buildings and projects, including marketing and leasing as well as building management; and

□ Funds management to raise and invest capital for development.

Gerald Hines conceived of and helped fund a ULI student urban design competition. Shown here (top) is the 2003 team from the University of Southern California and (bottom) Hines observing the students' presentations, with William Alsup (left) of the Hines organization and James Kostaras, a faculty adviser from Harvard University.

A major advantage of such a broadly based organization is the capability it gives for adjusting to ups and downs in the marketplace. Jeff Hines observes that when the market dropped in the early 1990s, the development business evaporated, leaving his company the choice either of hibernating or of building on its expertise to expand into other areas of real estate. It chose the latter course, shifting its focus to investment, acquisition of existing assets, asset management—including reclaiming buildings for resale—and increasing its third-party, build-to-suit activities. Hines took on development management for educational facilities and medical buildings. It became a financial adviser and co-investor. During the lull in the U.S. market, the company also moved aggressively to develop in foreign nations, setting up offices (after exhaustive market evaluations) in places where they could expect to operate for 20 or 30 years.

In addition to producing good-looking buildings, Hines emphasizes that the company's development products are good for the client's employees. Tenant satisfaction is the goal in design and property management. Jeff Hines makes the point that property management is not just a commodity. "There is a quality of care and attention to detail," he says, "that on-site engineers and managers are proud of, and the benefit to tenants is clear."ˣˣⁱ For Hines, the object of building is not just creating a pretty face but to lower maintenance costs while keeping tenants comfortable and hassle-free. On a day-to-day basis, Hines's on-site professional managers use a software program to identify recurring problems, address requests promptly, track response time, and determine the best distribution of resources. In addition, to anticipate tenant needs, Hines uses its expertise to foster new building design, operation, and management standards.

The Hines design team considers every aspect of building design and systems at the conceptual phase of project development, exploring and evaluating alternatives. Once selections are made, comparative analyses with applications in competitive buildings are carried out. The Hines people also thoroughly test innovations before adopting them. Because of its buying power, Hines has

Completed in 1999 on a ten-acre site in Bellevue, Washington, Cedar Court is a campus-style complex comprising four office buildings totaling 428,400 square feet. In November 2002, the Cedar Court development was sold to Microsoft, which is now the single-tenant user. Architect: G2 Architecture.

found manufacturers willing to test applications of new equipment to provide the company with a forecast of product performance prior to purchase and use.

To measure tenants' satisfaction with a building, Hines engages independent firms to survey occupants every year, using the results as benchmarking data to ensure that clients' concerns are being addressed. Improvements to building systems promote green building, as discussed in an earlier section, but also make a difference to tenants, holding their interest in remaining in the building.

Hines himself is a full-service man, fascinated by all aspects of real estate development in business and in public. He has served on the usual roster of city and organizational boards but has made two important contributions to bettering the process of community development. He helped establish the Gerald Hines Professorship in Real Estate Finance at Rice University, and he has served as an outstanding patron to the University of Houston School of Architecture, which has been renamed in his honor the Gerald D. Hines School of Architecture at the University of Houston. Hines also declined his J.C. Nichols prize money and provided a matching amount to fund the ULI Gerald D. Hines Student Urban Design Competition, "to raise awareness of high-quality urban design in creating buildings and living environments."

Downtown Denver's Wells Fargo Center, completed in 1983, is a 50-story, 1.27 million-square-foot office tower of russet-colored granite and gray glass. Architect: Johnson/ Burgee Architects.

A MATTER OF DETERMINATION

The story of Hines's success could be said to boil down to a determination to build the best. Making money is certainly one motivation but Gerald Hines repeatedly uses the word "challenge" to explain his and his company's driving force. His determination to excel is reflected in his appetite for physical exertion. His friends know him as a skilled athlete and intense competitor—a participant in rather than an observer of sports. He ran track in high school and college and then became an avid golfer and tennis player. But he stepped up his activities after being diagnosed in the early 1980s with coronary heart disease. Rather than submit to a heart bypass, he chose to change his diet and commence a strenuous exercise program. Like anything he undertakes, he found top-notch instruction and then worked to become an expert. He plays tennis or bikes 20

miles almost every day, runs up and down mountains and takes long cross-country treks, and avidly pursues perfection in golf. While residing part-time at Aspen over the years, he took up skiing, snowboarding, in-line skating, and mountain biking. And amazingly, while the years go by he keeps at it. At 79, he says that between Aspen and the Alps he skied 46 days last year. That's determination, and that describes Hines's approach to everything he does.

NOTES

i Philip Johnson, Hilary Lewis, and John T. O'Connor, *Philip Johnson in His Own Words* (New York: Rizzoli, 1994), p. 128.

ii Patricia Busa McConnico, "Gerald Hines," *Texas Monthly Biz,* September 2000 (downloaded from www.texasmonthly.com).

iii SS&C Technologies, Inc., *Skyline,* November 15, 2002.

iv Johnson et al., *Philip Johnson,* p. 128.

v *Handbook of Texas Online,* www.tsha.utexas.edu, May 4, 2004, p. 8.

vi This and other quotations of Philip Johnson's in this paragraph were drawn from Johnson et al., *Philip Johnson,* pp. 118–122.

vii Paul Heyer, *American Architecture: Ideas and Ideologies in the Late Twentieth Century* (New York: John Wiley & Sons, 1993), p. 128.

viii Johnson et al., *Philip Johnson,* p. 126.

ix Jana J. Madsen, "The Secret to Hines' Success," *Buildings,* November 2003, p. 4.

x Ibid., p. 3.

xi Cynthia J. Hoffman, "Turning Risk Into Reward," *Real Estate Forum,* August 1998.

xii Ibid.

xiii Madsen, "The Secret to Hines' Success," p. 2.

xiv Daniel Fisher, "Second Empire," *Forbes,* October 30, 2000.

xv Ibid.

xvi Madsen, "The Secret to Hines' Success."

xvii Hoffman, "Turning Risk Into Reward."

Biking is one of Hines's many athletic hobbies.

xviii Ibid.

xix Fisher, "Second Empire."

xx Hoffman, "Turning Risk into Reward."

xxi Madsen, "The Secret to Hines' Success."

PRIMARY REFERENCES

Fisher, Daniel. "Second Empire." *Forbes*, October 30, 2000.

Hoffman, Cynthia J. "Turning Risk Into Reward." *Real Estate Forum,* August 1998.

Johnson, Philip, Hilary Lewis, and John T. O'Connor. *Philip Johnson: The Architect in His Own Words.* New York: Rizzoli, 1994.

Madsen, Jana J. "The Secret to Hines' Success." *Buildings,* November 2003.

Urban Land Institute. "The Galleria, Houston, Texas." *Project Reference File,* Urban Land Institute, vol. 1, no. 9, 1971.

Handbook of Texas Online. www.tsha.utexas.edu. May 4, 2004.

"Shell Plaza Towers." *Emporis Buiding Database.* www.emporis.com. May 8, 2004.

AUTHOR INTERVIEWS

Jan de Kreij, chief executive officer, Corio NV, April 2004, by telephone.

Gerald D. Hines, chairman, Hines, June 2004, by telephone.

Jeffrey C. Hines, president, Hines, May 2004, by telephone.

Robert Hollister, vice president, Hines Seattle office, May 2004, by telephone.

Robert A.M. Stern, dean, Yale School of Architecture, May 2004, by telephone.

Michael Topham, executive vice president, Hines Europe Regional office, May 2004, by telephone.

[A]RCHITECTURE IS A COMMUNAL ART, HAVING TO DO WITH THE
WHOLE MANMADE ENVIRONMENT, THE HUMAN CITY ENTIRE, RATHER
THAN ONLY THE INDIVIDUAL BUILDINGS WITHIN IT.
VINCENT SCULLY, "AMERICA AT THE MILLENNIUM:
ARCHITECTURE AND COMMUNITY"[1]

VINCENT SCULLY

VISIONARY TEACHER, WRITER, ADVOCATE

VINCENT SCULLY REMEMBERS WALKING around his New Haven neighborhood as a boy, looking at houses and trying to understand how the rooms were arranged. Decades later, he wrote of Frank Lloyd Wright's Heurtley House: "[It] opened up the box . . . so that it draws us into it. It is at once secret, dark, and concealing, profoundly primitive and brooding in aspect but also inviting, leading us by tortuous ways into its enfolding body: cavern, pavilion, and castle all at once."[ii] Scully's childhood wonderings about building spaces and functions had blossomed into a lifetime fascination with the spatial qualities of architecture and their contributions to nurturing human environments. In his book *Modern Architecture,* he quoted architect Louis Kahn: "A city is a place where a small boy, as he walks through it, may see something that will tell him what he wants to do his whole life."[iii]

Today, Scully is revered as an inspiring teacher, prolific writer, and advocate of what he terms "the architecture of community." During the 60-plus years of his career, he has incisively changed the ways that generations of architects and urban designers think about buildings and their settings and, through their work, the form and quality of our communities. Rarely are historians credited with affecting the course of urban development, but Scully's upbringing, education, and nimble intellectual prowess have made him uniquely persuasive in conveying his particular grasp of socially conscious urban design.

GROWING UP IN NEW HAVEN AND YALE

Vincent Scully was born in 1920, the only child of Irish Catholic parents, in New Haven, Connecticut.[iv] New Haven, with Yale University, became the setting for his entire life. Scully's father, a car salesman with a passion for reading, became a Democratic alderman for the city government and was elected president of the board of aldermen. His mother was a classic coloratura soprano whose voice, he ruefully records, he found painfully piercing as a child. (To this day, Scully has little to do with music, a peculiarity in a man whose vocation centers on an art form that Goethe likened to "frozen music.")

They lived in a two-family house—the classic New Haven two-decker with a front gable—one family down and one up. Scully recalls no other children his age on the street. The family belied the Irish Catholic stereotype by having a small household and few friends or visitors. He told James Stevenson of the *New Yorker*, "[I] had a real sense of having nobody, and that marked my whole life. It made me melancholy but liberated. I had to figure it all out for myself." Those feelings may have been influenced by his mother's death when he was 15 years old. (His father lived to age 85.)

Books, however, were plentiful in his home and Scully learned to read in his preschool years. He played with Lincoln Logs and electric trains with model houses; his parents were generous with toys until the Great Depression ruined his father's business. As he grew older, Scully frequented the New Haven Free Public Library, borrowing four or five books, reading them in a couple of days, and returning for more. At 16, having skipped two grades, he entered Yale on a full scholarship.

His experience in his Yale undergraduate years was a mixed bag. Scully describes his confusion about what career to follow. Feeling unsettled and unfocused, he spent many afternoons in the library reading P.G. Wodehouse and Evelyn Waugh, and in movie theaters. To this day, his memory can dredge up the story lines and principal actors of dozens of movies made in the 1930s and 1940s. He also played intramural football and was on the fencing team. In the academic realm, however, he discovered an interest in the French language and literary criticism. Then he took a course in art history that "opened up the floodgates," pointing to the direction of future interests.v He graduated as an English major in 1940.

Thinking graduate school a natural next step, Scully enrolled in Yale's English department. Still seeking a sense of direction, he left after one class to join the Army Air Corps. When he failed to make the grade as a flyer, he joined the Marine Corps, subsequently spending five years as a Marine infantry officer in the Mediterranean and Pacific theaters. His major recollection from this experience is catching his first glimpse of Italy and a Greek temple or two as an offshore observer during the invasion of Sicily.

Eager to tackle graduate school on returning to Yale in 1946, Scully decided to work toward a doctorate in art history at one of the most distinguished departments in the nation. It was dominated by a French tradition that emphasized the changing meanings of forms over time and their effect on the viewer's direct visual experience, a perspective that became a guiding principle of Scully's teachings and writings. To Scully, it was a commonsensical contrast to the doctrinaire new criticism of Yale's English department, with its alienating insistence on the autonomy of the work and on "the words themselves." His intellectualism flourished in the art history department, and in a way his later theories about Greek temples, Native American pueblos, and classical French gardens could be seen as a repudiation of the confining principles of the new criticism.

A year and a half into graduate work, he began teaching a survey course in art history and a special course on modern architecture for architects. As preparation for the latter, he took a course in architectural design that brought him into close contact with architects.

A deepening interest in the built environment led to his selection of a dissertation topic, an aspect of architectural history remote from the preconceptions of academia but literally close to home: 19th-century vernacular design, particularly of houses. Scully aimed to reawaken an appreciation of American domestic architecture of the past century, which he regarded as a neglected subject often dismissed in intellectual circles as unimportant or, worse, bad taste. Henry-Russell Hitchcock, the dean of modern architectural historians in America and author of definitive treatises on H. H. Richardson and Frank Lloyd Wright, served as his adviser and remained his mentor for many years. Scully's dissertation—"The Cottage Style: An Organic Development in Later Nineteenth-Century Wooden Domestic Architecture in the Eastern United States"—according to Neil Levine, constituted a "new and ultimately definitive explanation for the evolution of premodern architecture in the United States" from the late 1840s to the advent of Frank Lloyd Wright's work at the century's end.[vi]

The president of Yale, Richard Levin, wrote: [Scully has done] more than it is imaginable one Eli ever could do—"For City, For Country, and For Yale."

Commenting later on his choice of a dissertation topic, Scully observed that it allowed him to undertake most of his research in the Yale library without traveling to foreign climes, which, in those pre-Fulbright days, he could not afford. Besides, the domestic architectural style was a familiar one. He had grown up in a house that displayed many characteristics of vernacular design: one built sometime in the late 1800s on a narrow lot, clad with clapboard and shingles, boasting projecting bays and gables decorated with scrolls, and graced with a small, two-story front porch—one of rows of similar houses along the street. (The house on Derby Avenue still exists.)

Scully completed his dissertation a mere three-and-a-half years after beginning graduate work, an accomplishment that reflects only part of his scholarly endeavors. During that period he also published his first article, about architecture as a science; participated as a panelist with a roster of world-famous architects in a symposium called "What Is Happening to Modern Architecture?"; and became acquainted with Louis Kahn and Philip Johnson, destined to become iconic figures in the architectural profession. Through Hitchcock, he also met Frank Lloyd Wright, whose work he admired, and in mid-1947 visited Taliesin in Wisconsin to see Wright's major buildings. (Scully also asked Wright to design a house for him and his wife but then found, to the dismay and resentment of Wright's apprentices, that he could not afford to build it. Scully went on to design his own home, which remained his first and only published work of design.)

Scully: It [teaching] comes naturally to me. . . . Here's an audience that listens, that pretends to be interested, that reacts and responds, and you have a dialogue. It's better than psychoanalysis.

SCULLY AS TEACHER AND MENTOR

Scully moved directly into the teaching mainstream with his appointment at Yale as a full-time faculty member in the history of art in 1949. He taught and, at 84, still teaches courses on the history of art and architecture in addition to lecturing on modern architecture. In time, he established a legendary reputation as a mesmerizing lecturer.

He draws parallels between ancient and modern art and architecture but ranges widely over the intellectual landscape, citing the writings of novelists and poets, referring to mythic and religious concepts, suggesting relationships among objects and cultures, opening up intellectual vistas for students, most of whom came from literary rather than visually oriented backgrounds. His classes at Yale are always full to overflowing. In 1966, *Time* magazine included Scully as one of the ten "great teachers" in the United States; in 1975, *People* magazine recognized him as one of the "12 great U.S. professors."

Scully's teaching style may echo that of a mentor he had during his undergraduate years, Chauncey Brewster Tinker. Tinker's flowery and rhetorical presentations made him a popular lecturer on 18th-century English and the romantic poets. Scully remembers his clear intelligence combined with "a finicky elegance and a persnickety wit" that were highly suited to his subject. It was Tinker who got Scully back into graduate school after the war.

In appearance, Scully seems chosen by central casting as the consummate Ivy League professor: a big man, fit-looking (he still rows in all seasons on the Branford River and the canals of Coral Gables), a somewhat weather-beaten face, a full head of gray hair, an energetic air on the podium. He speaks rapidly, without notes. Scully makes his lectures a whole-body experience, jabbing at details on the slide screens, raising his arms to sketch enclosed spaces, sweeping a hand to indicate the long views, turning from the screen to fix his eyes on a front-row student to emphasize a point. And on to the next slide. Meanwhile, he commands whole-mind attention, pointing out a dozen details on the slides before him—spaces and vistas, functions and meanings, facade treatments and structural details—then leaps to provocative generalizations that link back to antecedents and forward to shifts in design ideas. Witticisms and whimsical sidebars are sprinkled throughout.

Robert F. Thompson, a fellow art history professor at Yale, described Scully's influence on students: "It takes courage to go up there and lecture day after day, wringing yourself dry, giving everything you've got at the highest intellectual, and even spiritual, level. A lot of his students have caught fire from his sun, taken some of that solar gaseous stuff and spun their own galaxies."[vii] Elizabeth Plater-Zyberk, once one of his teaching assistants, observes, "He is the only historian I know who truly understands how an architect designs—the psyche and the process—and thus insinuates himself into the production of design." She adds: "He opens up a whole new world, challenges students to do better than the works he's describing, and sends them out into the world aching to do great things."

Scully: The teacher is the most fortunate of men, so long as he allows himself to be taught.

Scully received tenure in 1956 and the rank of full professor five years later. In 1983, he was named the Sterling Professor of the History of Art at Yale. But Yale's rules forced Scully to retire from full-time teaching as the school year ended in 1991, when he turned 70. Many of the architects he had taught or influenced, such as Philip Johnson, Maya Lin, Cesar Pelli, Kevin Roche, and Robert A.M. Stern, attended his final lecture, considered enough of a story to win a front-

ARCHITECTS, SCHOLARS, CRITICS, CITY PLANNERS, PRESERVATIONISTS, URBANITES, AND THOSE WHO PASSED THROUGH HIS CLASS WHO HAD NEVER CONNECTED DIRECTLY TO THESE FIELDS—BECAUSE OF VINCE, THEY BECAME BETTER CLIENTS, MORE CIVILIZED BANKERS, MAYBE EVEN MORE HONORABLE POLITICIANS. PAUL GOLDBERGER, ARCHITECTURE CRITIC

Robert A.M. Stern: Scully has taught us that we need not be embarrassed to be American architects . . . [and that] American culture [has] its own dignity and even grandeur.

page spot in the *New York Times* the following Sunday. It did not take long for Scully to adjust to retirement. Although he continues as an emeritus professor to teach at Yale in the fall term, alternating from year to year the course in modern architecture with the introduction to art history, he began teaching at the University of Miami in the spring of 1992 as distinguished visiting professor in the architecture school. Andrés Duany and Elizabeth Plater-Zyberk—dean of the architecture school at Miami—both well known in new urbanist circles, succeeded in

HE ILLUMINATED THE TRAJECTORY OF AMERICAN ARCHITECTURE AS A WORTHY AND RICH CULTURAL FOUNDATION FOR CONTEMPORARY INVENTION. HOW MANY OF US CAME OF AGE AS DESIGNERS DETERMINED TO CARRY ON THE TRADITIONS OF AMERICAN ARCHITECTURE SO GLORIOUSLY EXPOSED IN VINCE'S LECTURES. ELIZABETH PLATER-ZYBERK, ARCHITECT

attracting Scully and his art historian wife, Catherine Lynn, to join the faculty. His lectures during the spring semester in Miami continue to lure and stimulate students, as they do in the fall semester in New Haven.

SCULLY AS ARCHITECTURAL HISTORIAN

Immediately upon receiving his Ph.D., Scully began his incredibly productive writing and publishing career—an essential part of every professor's intellectual development and influence. But Scully's Irish heritage seems to speak through his passionate writing as in his spoken word. He admits to finding writing difficult at first, but he learned through constantly self-editing his lively style and expressive vocabulary—what he calls his "gnarled prose."

He first launched into publishing the results of his dissertation research, celebrating the indigenous creativity demonstrated by the

exploitation of materials and spatial forms in American vernacular architecture. He contributed two chapters on the stick and shingle styles of architecture to the book *The Architectural Heritage of Newport, Rhode Island, 1640–1915,* published in 1952. A year later, the *Art Bulletin* published the first chapter of his dissertation, and in 1954, Scully published an article summarizing his dissertation ideas in the prestigious *British Architectural Review*. In 1955, Scully realized every Ph.D.'s dream when the Yale University Press published a somewhat truncated version of his dissertation—titled *The Shingle Style: Architectural Theory and Design from Richardson to the Origins of Wright*—to considerable acclaim, including the Art Historical Award of the College Art Association. By then, Scully's defini-

tions of the "stick" style of visible structure and the "shingle" style of surfacing the created space were becoming widely accepted and respected as expressions of American domestic design. Later, in his preface to the 1971 revised edition (in which Scully reinserted a discussion of the stick style, which had been dropped in the first edition), he touched on the deep meaning of the stick and shingle housing styles for Americans: "Regarded purely as architecture, those houses were surely even better than I thought they were when I wrote about them, and they have proved to be even more important in a historical sense and as the inspiration of new architecture."[viii]

Meanwhile, Scully pursued other interests that soon merged into the central theme of his scholarship: the significance of context in architecture. A Fulbright Fellowship awarded in 1950 would have taken him to France to study Gothic architecture. It was deferred due to teaching duties and when Scully left for Europe the following year, it was to Italy to examine the relationships between cities and the environment. Scully later said the opportunity to visit ancient Roman sites, the medieval Italian cities and hill towns, and, most significantly, the Greek temples at Paestum, was "the central event of my intellectual life."[ix] He saw and wrote about Michelangelo's fortification drawings. The Ambrogio Lorenzetti fresco *The Allegory of Good Government in Siena* provided a vision of how towns should function and relate to their natural environments. The setting of the

KEVIN GLOWACKI

PHILIP GREENSPUN

Greek temples within their landscapes impressed him as integral to their meaning.

Scully felt deeply enough about the significance of his observations abroad to spend the summer of 1955 in Greece, the summer of 1956 in southern Italy and Sicily, and, with a Bollingen Foundation grant, the entire academic year of 1957–1958 in Greece. As an associate of the American School of Classical Studies in Athens, he completed the research and most of the writing for *The Earth, the Temple, and the Gods: Greek Sacred Architecture,* published in 1962. Scully perceived that the eyes of archeologists studying ancient building sites— "a moldy bunch," he once said[x]—were fixed on the ground, while the landscapes rising around the sites were ignored. His thesis was that Greek temples (and by extension, other emblematic buildings) "needed to be looked at afresh in terms of their own forms and meaning and in relation to those of the landscapes in which they were set."[xi]

With his studies of Greek temples and Amerindian pueblos, Scully moved his emphasis from the building as object to the building in context.

He compared his response to the Greek temples to the moment when Herman Melville, author of *Moby Dick*, mounted the Acropolis of Athens in 1857: "[H]e was able to understand all at once the miracle of reconciliation between men and nature which rose before his eyes. A white presence stood before him, high on its platform of rock above the long view to the sea. The cones and horns of the mountains lay behind it, fixed by its solemn permanence but uncompromised by it, and around it the whole horizon swung in a single arc."[xii]

The book inspired by Scully's trip to New Mexico demonstrated a similar concern with the relationship between buildings and settings. *Pueblo: Mountain, Village, Dance,* published in 1975, described how pueblos of the Southwest echo the forms of the surrounding landscape rather than contrast with them, as do Greek temples. It is an architecture meant to accommodate rather than confront nature. Scully concentrated, as he did with the Greek temples, on observations and descriptions of buildings in their landscape settings, but because ritual dances and ceremonies were still performed in the pueblos, he enlarged his focus to account for their meaning as well. Scully labored over describing this complex equation of building, nature, and ceremony for six years.

Scully's historical synthesis of these concepts, together with ideas about town planning flowing from his later study of French classical gardens, came in *Architecture: The Natural and the Man-made,* a 1991 book also published in condensed form in a number of journals. The grand sweep of this book is evident in the opening sentence of the essay: "The way human beings see themselves in relation to nature is fundamental to all cultures; thus the first fact of architecture is the natural world, the second is the relationship of human structures to the topography of the world, and the third is the relationship of all these structures to each other, comprising the human community as a whole."[xiii] He observed the threat that human structures pose to the natural environment and the failure of "modern" architecture to work out relationships to nature. The prominence he gave to the planning of French classical gardens foretold his growing support for neotraditionalist urban design.

SCULLY AS CRITIC

During all these years, Scully continued his outpouring of articles and essays, many leading to, drawn from, or further elaborating chapters of his books, and others commentaries on various current topics. As a historian, Scully identified the strands of architectural theory and practice that combined to form specific approaches to design, including the modern movement. But a second major theme of his work, one seen by many as his most important contribution to the architectural profession, centered on critiques of contemporary architecture. As a critic, he evaluates the structures, spaces, and materials of modern buildings as art forms and probes their contributions to the quality of human existence. To accomplish these ends, besides his extensive scholarship in historic literature, he has cultivated wide acquaintances and friendships among contemporary architects, tested out ideas in conversations and forums, analyzed the design features of new and old buildings through on-site visits and/or study of drawings and photographs, and written numerous essays and books to explain his views.

From his first explorations of American architecture, Scully admired Frank Lloyd Wright's work as an early and instrumental influence on the forms of modern architecture. Wright worked during the late 1880s and early 1890s in Chicago, where he found fertile ground for experimenting with creating discipline, clarity, and order in domestic architecture. Scully traced the influence on Wright of the spatial concepts of American architects, including the early designs of McKim, Mead & White. He found that Wright mastered the interweaving of spatial areas within a total design, commenting: "Wright intensifies, extends, and clarifies" the experience of the time.[xiv] Wright's influence on modern architecture was expanded when, in 1910, Ernst Wasmuth published a large volume of Wright's drawings (and another a year later) and an exhibition of his work was mounted in Berlin. Scully quoted Mies on the immense effect in Europe of these events: "The work of this great master presented an architectural world of unexpected force, clarity of language, and disconcerting richness of form. Here, finally, was a master-builder drawing upon the veritable fountainhead of architecture. . . . The dynamic impulse emanating from his work invigorated a whole generation."[xv] Scully credited Wright's work as a vital force in the eventual formation of the international style by such architects as Mies and Le Corbusier. The reverse flow of European designs by these masters and others, Scully concluded, influenced Wright's later designs for projects such as Fallingwater.

Frank Lloyd Wright's Robie House (Chicago, 1910) may have been a seminal work of architecture as object, but Scully believed that its premise was antithetical to the urban context.

Scully's analysis of Wright's work and influence illustrates his role as an architecture critic. He delves into the mind of the architect to discover what he or she was attempting to create, and why; to convey a sense of the structure's massing, spaces, and materials; and to evaluate whether the creator has achieved his or her aims. He also seeks to understand the way the architect seizes on opportunities or overcomes limitations presented by the nature of the site and the physical or financial resources at hand.

Scully believes in the visual experience of architecture as individual works of art. But he is particularly concerned with discerning how structures speak to the human condition—how they shelter, protect, gratify, or evoke inspirational perceptions, for example. He translates the language of architectural design—the sticks and stones and spaces—to convey the way

they shape spaces and views, offer warmth and delight.

Scully described Frank Lloyd Wright's Johnson Wax headquarters in Racine, Wisconsin, to his class at the University of Miami, pointing to the slide screens:

> "Johnson Wax is Wright's masterpiece. Here are what Wright called the 'lilypads.' Wright has these slender columns reaching up, then swelling out to support the ceiling—but looking as if they were growing up from the bottom like water lilies, floating above, too pliant to support anything. We look up from the floor as from the bottom of a pool. A neo-Bauhaus architect once said that he could bridge that space with one beam and a philosopher found them 'excessive for typists.' But look at the space they create—walking into that room you float up in the pool, a strange and dreamlike sensation. You are a child of the water, a magical being calmer than mankind, outside time. 'Excessive for typists' indeed."

One of Scully's first critical essays dealing specifically with modern architecture, "Archetype and Order in Recent American Architecture," appeared in *Art in America* in 1954. He found that American architecture was reviving classical forms, proportions, and the unity of the structure as a whole. He saw a desire for a "few strongly contrasted shapes with decisive details," which, he believed, reflect the yearning for direct and simple experience in an increasingly complex world.[xvi] Scully singled out Mies as the exemplar of this trend, with designs such as those for the Illinois Institute of Technology and the Lakeshore Apartments, both in Chicago. But others active in pursuing these ends, he said, include architects such as Eero Saarinen, Paul Rudolph, Louis Kahn, Paul Schweikher, and Philip Johnson. (All have been associated, either as students or as lecturers, with the Yale School of Architecture, and their work contrasts with the design concepts of the Harvard-based, neo-Bauhaus school that Scully has always felt were "regressive and repressive.")

Scully observed that Philip Johnson's New Canaan houses, for example, express the archetypal sensations of enclosure and release. The Wiley House, in particular, in its juxtaposition of shelter and natural space, "is a small, contained temple in the landscape." The 1954 essay ended with the magisterial conclusion that contemporary architects are "profoundly determined to create those experiences by forms which can be thoroughly controlled and integrally detailed in all their parts . . . leading to a renewed interest in Renaissance and antique systems of proportion and of columnar and vaulted structures."

LOUIS SLOVINSKY

As a critic of architecture as art, Scully saw the work of Philip Johnson—such as his infamous Glass House (New Canaan, Connecticut, 1949)—as an advancement in the international style.

Just three years after this was written, Scully presented his ideas on the development of the modern style in an essay titled "Modern Architecture: Toward a Redefinition of Style." The essay (just a dozen pages) was revised and expanded into the book *Modern Architecture: The Architecture of Democracy,* published in 1961. It is still in print after more than 40 years as one of the most authoritative publications on the subject. At the outset of the essay, Scully cautioned that the ambiguous concept of "style" should be accepted as "a body of work exhibiting family resemblances"[xvii] rather than one insisting on hard-and-fast rules. He proposed that modern architecture must acknowledge the idea of democracy as the fundamental social force of the era. The "architecture of democracy"—a phrase originated by Frank Lloyd Wright—Scully said has been evolving from the breakup of the baroque style, through the continuity of design and new respect for classicism embodied in the international style, to a new humanism such as the imagistic, bodily form of expression found in Le Corbusier's Ronchamp chapel and his other postwar work. Scully wrote, ". . . [W]e cannot look at Ronchamp without considering the capacity of architecture to function as sculptural presence." In comparison to the Parthenon, Ronchamp "is at once more complicated, more primitive, and more impatient, like modern humanity."

By the end of the 1960s, however, Scully appeared disenchanted with modern architecture. Much of what was wrong he blamed on Walter Gropius, who arrived at Harvard in the late 1930s and "brought with him most of the few weaknesses and few of the many virtues" that his Bauhaus work had possessed.[xviii] Scully believed that Gropius, as an influential teacher and leader of the neo-Bauhaus movement, had misled modern architecture. In *American Architecture and Urbanism,* published in 1969, Scully chastised American architects for borrowing European forms primarily for their picturesque possibilities while dismissing the urbanist, social, and rational underpinnings of these forms espoused by European architects.

A decade later, answering the question posed in his essay titled "Where is Modern Architecture Going?" Scully lamented the state of contemporary architecture in no uncertain terms. Modern architecture, he said, is "surely the dreariest archetype for an urban architecture that human history has so far recorded. . . . [It] is an environmentally destructive mass of junk, dominated by curtain-wall corporate structures which will continue to be built so long as modern bureaucracy exists."[xix] Commenting on an exhibition of modern buildings at New York's Museum of Modern Art, Scully was depressed by the "mindless profusion of a grab-bag of aggressively maladjusted, primitive, and crippled forms." When it became a reality rather than a dream, said Scully, "The limitations of modern architecture became rapidly apparent, as growing numbers of modern buildings began to destroy the complex urban structure." Modern design was especially incapable of creating "an environment either adequately articulated or properly unified."

While individual architects such as Saarinen and Alvar Aalto produced designs of expressive sensibility, said Scully, the work of many contemporary architects from the 1950s into the 1970s veered between heavy monumentality to poorly realized revivals of Renaissance designs, too often celebrating technological innovations for packaging space while creating empty interior landscapes and jarring relationships to surrounding structures. And when they did create so-called masterpieces, such as the Lever House and Seagram Building in New York City, the buildings failed to maintain the quality of the street—Park Avenue—on which their prestigious address depended. In "The Death of the Street," based on a 1961 talk, Scully engaged publicly for the first time the issue of urbanism and the concept of contextualism. Writing as the Pan American Building was being completed, he lamented the impact of the modern glass skyscraper as a "blind destructive force eroding the very street fabric" it needs to meet its commercial ends.[xx] Scully perceived that the freestanding presence of the new buildings along Park Avenue fractured the space-defining character of its eclectic assortment of buildings. Mostly contiguous, establishing a solid frontage on the street, they provided a civil framework for urban life. Although one building such as the Lever House might have been an adornment for Park Avenue, he said, the succession of buildings conceived as independent monuments to the self-centered talent of their architects punched holes in the wall of the street. Moreover, what he described as the "fat, wide slab" of the Pan American Building blocked the view down the avenue beyond Grand Central Station and overwhelmed its scale.

In 1980, in his essay "Where Is Modern Architecture Going?" however, Scully saw hope in the work of Robert Venturi in the United States and the neorationalists such as Aldo Rossi in Europe. The latter, he said, adopt a stern resolve to revive and simplify the forms of the international style of the 1920s, reducing architecture to its geometric essentials. Though neorationalism is wedded to pure form, it specifically recognizes the significance of urban patterns of development and tends to hark back to some aspects of vernacular styles. Scully believed that neorationalism would appeal to the academic establishment but he, himself, at that time, preferred Venturi's emphasis on vernacular design, picking up aspects of the shingle style but also borrowing from contempo-

Scully championed the work of Robert Venturi—such as his Vanna Venturi house (Philadelphia, 1962)—as having both architectural and urbanistic merit.

rary American commercial strip developments. (Later, though, he was especially moved by the "haunting, timeless" quality of Rossi's design.) Said Scully, Venturi "conceptualized and formed architecture in the simplest possible way as an affair of 'decorated sheds' of well-proportioned buildings," shaped by their functions and decorated rather playfully with devices that embody their meaning.[xxi] Scully perceived that Venturi meant to adapt, clarify, and generally abstract the basic vernacular forms, changing their scale and sometimes parodying them.

Venturi's first important building was his mother's house built in 1964 in the Chestnut Hill neighborhood of Philadelphia. In his 1966 essay "Robert Venturi's Gentle Architecture," Scully called it "disarmingly simple," based on a symbolic rather than a purely spatial concept. From a central tall chimney the interior space is "pulled" from the hearth. The split gable over the front door rises, "opens, lifts, making the house sculpturally active."[xxii] In "Everybody Needs Everything," which revisited the initial analysis of the house a quarter-century later, Scully said, "Surely there never was a building so in love with the complexities and contradictions of architecture. . . ."[xxiii] Scully went on to praise the house as "the biggest small building of the second half of the twentieth century." (This essay demonstrated his fascination with Venturi's design skills. In it, Scully traced the evolution and meanings of six separate schemes for the building, preserved in a remarkable collection of drawings that Venturi had worked up before finalizing the design. He showed how Venturi worked incrementally toward a spatial economy and unity to produce spaces that flowed internally, a design "spiritually simple, certain, and strong. . . .")

MODERN ARCHITECTS WISHED TO BE FREE OF ANY RESTRAINTS BY THE URBAN CONTEXT, FREE TO RIP THE OLD URBANISM APART OR TO OUTRAGE IT . . . OR TO USE ITS ORDER, WHILE IT LASTED, AS A BACKGROUND BEFORE WHICH THEY COULD CAVORT.
VINCENT SCULLY, "THE ARCHITECTURE OF COMMUNITY"

SCULLY AS URBANIST

For Scully, the villains in the modern architecture movement were what he came to call the "hero-architects," who chose to ignore the setting of their creations in the quest for fame. In his essay "Architecture as Community," written in 1994 for Peter Katz's book *The New Urbanism: Toward an Architecture of Community,* Scully condemned architecture that disdains the very context that gives it life and goes against the grain of the city as the ultimate work of human art. Community was lost as the canons of modern architecture and planning in the mid-20th century turned against the city. Modern architects such as Wright, Le Corbusier, Mies, Gropius, and especially their followers, despised the traditional city—"the finest achievement of Western architecture, put together piece by piece over the centuries"—and were determined to replace it with their own personal, utopian, idiosyncratic schemes."[xxiv] Le Corbusier's Ville Radieuse, with its rows of bulky skyscrapers lined up along wide avenues, was the most influential, certainly as the model for much American redevelopment planning. At the other end of the scale, Wright's Broadacre City—equally destructive—celebrated low-density suburban design. Otherwise, the theme of the younger modern architects was individuality, and one could not make a community out of their buildings.

Scully said that there is a reason for this attitude: contextuality is difficult to achieve. In *American Architecture and Urbanism,* he wrote, ". . . contextuality demands a good deal of humility from the architect: he must respect what has gone before and subordinate the more egregious aspects of his own personality to it. How much more satisfying the Rambo role offered him by the international style: the past is junk, the architect is epic hero, reinventing the wheel every time."[xxv]

But Scully's disillusionment with modern architecture arose not just from the "maladjusted" products of hero-architects, but also from his taking umbrage at the destructive redevelopment going on in historic urban centers. The rending of the historic urban fabric is a subject close to home for Scully. From the 1960s

Whether Scully is teaching art or architectural history, his true worth as a teacher is in teaching urbanism.

onward, he inveighed against the redevelopment program undertaken by New Haven's city administration. Encouraged by a strong-minded mayor, the redevelopment agency wiped out thousands of homes for the poor in the center city—many more than it replaced. As distressing to Scully was construction of the first leg of a freeway bordered by frontage roads—hence a vast space bereft of buildings—"as if it were being laid out in the center of Nebraska rather than in a crowded city," said Scully.[xxvi] The redevelopment agency planned to border it with commercial buildings and a high-rise tower for elderly residents. Scully reported the results: neighborhoods broken up, the poor moving into increasingly crowded slums, and not too surprising, the 1967 riot that exploded in the "new" slums. Citizen pressure stopped the highway construction and stalemated further redevelopment. But the damage had been done; center-city communities were torn apart, leaving impoverished residents living in what Scully described as "a surreal wasteland with homes, churches, stores, and most of all the orienting street grid of the city, all shot to hell."[xxvii] Of the experience, Scully said, "The whole redevelopment thing politicized me, and I was very involved in the fight."[xxviii]

If modern architecture in urban settings and urban redevelopment programs in the 1960s raised sobering questions for Scully, architecture in the suburbs seemed to promise few solutions at that time. Scully saw the wave of suburbanization that occurred from the 1920s onward as the consequence of a specifically antiurban, antimonumental mindset that resulted in a small-scale, asymmetrical, two-dimensional type of design. In a sense, suburban architecture represented an

Once we built dignified places to live—a supporting community, like the pre–World War II Sunnyside Gardens in Queens. Scully believes we can do it again.

ALEXANDER GARVIN

escape from the larger questions of city building. It had little redeeming value for the fundamental needs of urban architecture.

True, some good work had been done in shaping suburban communities. Early in the 20th century, the garden cities movement fashioned by Ebenezer Howard in England, led to development of well-designed, pleasant suburban communities. A traditional command of charm and order characterized projects such as Forest Hills Gardens and Sunnyside Gardens on New York's Long Island. Somewhat later, and at a larger scale, new towns such as Columbia, Maryland, and Reston, Virginia, revived elements of that tradition but, Scully complained, city planners then tended to regard the typical street and its traffic as a danger to pedestrians, and planned major streets to separate rather than unite blocks of housing. Radburn, indeed, turned homes away from the street to face a central green. The Greenbelt towns of the 1930s followed these practices of separating homes from streets.

From that record of experience Scully concluded, "Despite the opinion of many distinguished American planners and critics, such as Lewis Mumford, the garden city and Le Corbusier's Villa Radieuse have many points of similarity," including their intention to "ream out the traditional density of the town and to destroy its streets." Later, Scully became much more sympathetic to the garden city, especially as it came to be associated in America with the city beautiful movement of the early 20th century. He has praised the urban results of that association not only in the leafy boulevards of that period—so preferable to the destructive connectors of the redevelopment era—but even more in the beautiful low-income neighborhoods built by the government as emergency wartime housing during World War I. He is pleased that some of his best students are now working on the largely misunderstood history and meaning of those movements.

Although Scully loathes automobiles (while admitting their usefulness), he believes they can be tamed by good urban design, making streets once more the central element of urban life that they have always been.[xxix] He made the point in a television discussion: "You can still have mobility, after all. You just don't have to create the environment so that the automobile is what shapes the whole environment."[xxx] The new urbanists, he suggested, have some reasonable answers about what to do with the automobile. They subject it, like all the other elements of the community, to reasonable laws.

SCULLY WAS AN EARLY, ARTICULATE, AND VOCAL CRITIC OF URBAN REDEVELOPMENT POLICIES, WHICH HE BLAMED FOR THE WHOLESALE DESTRUCTION OF INNER-CITY NEIGHBORHOODS. HE STOPPED PLANS TO REPLACE THE HISTORIC LIBRARY FACING NEW HAVEN'S GREEN, CAUSED A RETHINKING OF PROPOSALS TO REBUILD THE CITY HALL, AND, BESIDES STOPPING EXTENSION OF THE OAK STREET CONNECTOR, OPPOSED A PLAN TO BUILD A RING ROAD AROUND THE CITY. THIS WAS NOT JUST A BATTLE HERE OR THERE. FOR SCULLY IT WAS AN ONGOING PASSION. ROBERT A.M. STERN, ARCHITECT

SCULLY ON THE NEW URBANISM: THE ARCHITECTURE OF COMMUNITY

Venturi's importance for Scully was his intent to accommodate his designs to preexisting conditions, to create building forms and functions that made them integral parts of urban areas—the essence of contextualism. Scully has preached the contextual responsibilities of architectural design since his first trips to Italy and Greece. His critiques of the newest icons of architectural design always search for the ways they are integrated—or not integrated—with the landscapes and building masses around them. He wrote in 1991: "[T]he most important development of the past three decades or more has been the revival of the classical and vernacular traditions of architecture, which have always dealt with questions of community and environment, and their reintegration into the mainstream of modern architecture."[xxxi]

So it was not surprising that in the early 1990s Scully became an advocate of the new urbanism and its expression of traditional, vernacular, community-making principles of urban design. The new urbanism grew out of several influences absorbing the neotraditional style of residential design promoted by Andrés Duany and Elizabeth Plater-Zyberk (both students of Scully); the transit-oriented developments designed by Peter Calthorpe (also a Yale student) that are shaped by avenues that radiate from a village green around which civic and shopping buildings cluster; and the rebuilding of community through the renovation and reuse of historic buildings and neighborhoods espoused by the National Trust for Historic Preservation. The new urbanists propound the value of high densities and street systems that encourage walking and neighborliness; of pleasantly landscaped streets with closely spaced homes within walking distance of shopping, community services, transit stops, and green space; and of putting the automobile in its place on narrow streets and behind buildings.

[I]N ANY CITY, ARCHITECTURE BUILDS AN ENVIRONMENT WHICH NORMALLY TAKES SHAPE AND CHANGES ACROSS TIME, AND EVERYTHING . . . PLAYS A PART IN IT: BUILDINGS WITH INTERIOR FUNCTIONS AND EXTERIOR RESPONSIBILITIES, STREETS, SIDEWALKS, LIGHTS, SIGNS, AND AUTOMOBILES. VINCENT SCULLY, "RIBA DISCOURSE 1969: A SEARCH FOR PRINCIPLE BETWEEN TWO WARS"

In "The Architecture of Community," Scully described his delight in the reuse of vernacular styles and forms by Duany and Plater-Zyberk. They touted the domestic architecture of the late 19th and early 20th centuries, with building fronts close to the street, front porches, gables and turned posts, and garages on rear alleys. Scully related how the two budding architects showed his seminar students how effectively the older New Haven neighborhoods worked—how the small lots kept buildings close together, "the porches related to the street, the sidewalks with their picket fences and rows of trees bound the whole fabric together," and how the automobile could be disciplined.[xxxii]

Scully observed that, for Duany and Plater-Zyberk, the buildings come before the plan, because the buildings brought the New Haven grid into three dimensions to shape the space.

"It is not an architecture of individual buildings," he wrote in *Urbanities* in 1994, "lined up like paintings in a gallery, free of urban context. . . . It is an architecture of the community as a whole, architecture as it has always been—culture's basic stratagem, mediating between the individual and the terrors of nature's law."[xxxiii] Scully exulted, "For me, marinated in modernism, it was the revelation of a new life in everything. There was no reason whatever why the best of everything had to be consigned to the past. Everything was available to be used again; now, as always in architecture, there were models to go by, types to employ."[xxxiv]

The best-known example of the new urbanism is Seaside, a shoreline resort in Florida's panhandle. Andrés Duany and Elizabeth Plater-Zyberk began planning its development in 1979 and construction proceeded steadily through the early 1980s. Word of its unusual design spread throughout the architectural world during the mid-1980s and the popular press followed with significant coverage. Scully took the opportunity afforded by receiving an honorary degree from the University of Miami in 1990 to see the project for himself, and duly reported his impressions in the *New York Times* in January 1991.

Seaside, said Scully in "Architecture and Community," "has succeeded more fully than any other work of architecture in our time has done, in creating an image of community, a symbol of human culture's place in nature's vastness." The dense, three-dimensional arrangement of building types, grouped together on the shore of the Gulf of Mexico, presses close to the expanse of white sand and the blue sea. Scully reminded us of John Nolen's 1920s plan for Venice, Florida, whose grid system, broad hemicycles, and diagonal avenues can be seen in Seaside. Houses in Seaside cluster closely together and crowd the narrow streets, scaled more for pedestrians than cars. Especially fitting for a resort, many homes are fitted out with playful shapes and decorations. However, Scully scoffed at Duany and Plater-Zyberk's claim that they employ vernacular home designs due to their current popularity with clients, which he believes amounts to pandering to the "professional club" of architects. Vernacular styles are valid in themselves, he said, as are more modern architectural styles, when done right.

HIS THINKING HAS ALWAYS BEEN BASED ON THE NOTION THAT ARCHITECTURE IS NOT PURELY AESTHETICS, AND [ITS] REAL MEANING IS HOW IT CAN BE USED TO MAKE BETTER PLACES. HE HAS TAUGHT THE SOCIAL VALUE OF ARCHITECTURE. PAUL GOLDBERGER, ARCHITECTURE CRITIC

Robert Davis, Seaside's developer, was willing to take a chance, notes Scully. Developers, he said, always are open to ideas, although they want to make a profit. "It's when architects begin to think architecture is too important to pay attention to developers that they produce kitsch instead of great art."

Duany and Plater-Zyberk, however, went beyond designing the plan for development. Expecting that many of the houses in Seaside would be designed by other architects, they wrote a set of design requirements—essentially a detailed zoning code—to guide the three-dimensional form of future development. The code lays down specific requirements for building close to the front lot line, heights of buildings, sidewalk and street widths, open spaces, parking lot locations, and other elements of the site and neighborhood design. Scully admitted his initial reluctance to endorse the notion of placing design constraints on architects. But he was won over when he realized, "Architecture is fundamentally a matter not of individual buildings but of the shaping of community, and that, as in Paris, Uruk, or Siena, is done by the law."[xxxv]

Lacking a rigorous adherence to code strictures, similar developments have gone astray. Scully pointed to nearby developments that purport to imitate Seaside. The picket fences, gazebos, and vernacular architecture are there, he says, but the roads are too wide, the lots usually too big, and the density forgone so that the automobile still reigns and the sense of community is lost.

Also, the code does not guarantee architectural success. For example, a number of architects have designed Seaside homes with distinctly modern features; some have succeeded in adapting architectural elements to code requirements, making them part of the scene; others, according to Scully, have challenged the code, "as if originality were architecture's main virtue and subversion of community its greatest good." And for some, the temptation to overload structures with vernacular features has led to design anarchy—Scully has called some of the results "honky tonk." But Scully also draws a lesson from the expanding collection of good and not-so-good buildings: Seaside has the quality of not being perfect, and therefore is more interesting than the set pieces that some architects would prefer.

In "The Architecture of Community," Scully wrote that the new urbanism should really be labeled the new suburbanism. Not that such a title is a comedown, he said. The theme that courses through new urbanist principles is the redesign of the vast area in which most Americans live and where most development is taking place. Reshaping that sprawl of automobile-dependent suburbia into communities that make sense is a worthy goal in itself, without claiming the applicability of the principles to center cities as well as suburbs. New urbanist principles, he noted, did not yet deal with strategies for healing the ills of center cities, such as the historic preservation of in-city neighborhoods, a little farther out but still within city limits. Like any system of intellectual premises, Scully wrote, the new urbanism imposed restrictions on reality that do not fulfill all of the ideals of architecture.

Nevertheless, alluding to the criticism made by some that Seaside created resort homes for wealthy people, Scully hoped that the lessons of Seaside could be applied to the problem of housing for the poor in central cities. The poor need a community with the "five-minute walk" governing distances between neighborhood elements and building scales geared to the low-rise, suburban-sized environment that most Americans seem to want. Scully now cites the wonderful ways that new urbanist ideas (encouraged by Henry Cisneros in the early 1990s) have been adopted to shape the HOPE VI housing developments in many cities. Their scale and design quality, as well as the mix of household incomes they allow, improve opportunities for the poor formerly bottled up in dismal projects. He now regards the HOPE VI program as the most praiseworthy of the new urbanism's achievements, and deplores current efforts to starve it of funding.

Seaside—a model for the new urbanism— was planned by two students of Scully.

STEVEN BROOKE

Scully summed up his belief that the new urbanism is the most important development in contemporary architecture in a 1998 talk as part of the Millennium series at the White House, which was hosting the 20th annual Pritzker Architecture Prize award dinner.[xxxvi] While observing the admiration throughout the world of the individual, idiosyncratic, inventive architect, Scully reminded his audience, "Architecture is a communal art, having to do with the whole manmade environment, the human city entire, rather than only the individual buildings in it."[xxxvii] This view has political and artistic relevance, he said, touching on fundamental issues such as "the relation of freedom to order, of innovation to stability, and most of all the individual to

Scully decries the gutting of HOPE VI funding, which he credits with much that is praiseworthy in new urbanist projects, such as Peter Calthorpe's Henry Horner Homes (Chicago, 2001).

the law." Noting Jefferson's classical approach to designing buildings as contributions to making cities, then the loss of respect for classic forms in the destructive power of postwar redevelopment activities, Scully asserted, "Once upon a time, buildings and cities had been designed to get along with buildings from previous generations, creating places that outlast individual human lives." [xxxviii] In Scully's mind, the principle of context was seen as historically more important than style or originality. After all, he says, Hippodamus's plan for Miletus in the 5th century, B.C.E. said it all. The grid and agora combine and systematize the elements of the city. Those ideas flowed into the garden city and city beautiful plans—they aren't new. We don't need to reinvent them, as Le Corbusier tried to do, just recover them and use them as the basis for making towns.

Yet, Scully's vision contemplates that the integration of buildings within a town planned to form a community is one element of many that evolve from relationships between architecture and the natural environment—the subject of most of his life's research since his visits to Italy and Greece more than a half-century ago. After investigations of Southwest pueblos and French classical gardens, he spent much of the 1980s gradually assembling a sweeping historical synthesis of these ideas. His main train of thought is that architecture's proper goal is the shaping of the human environment within the natural world. Architecture is one of humanity's major strategies for mitigating the effects of nature's immutable laws on human beings. It shelters and reassures them. It mediates between the individual and the natural world, creating the physical structures that link individuals to the rest of humanity and that frame and tame nature.

The revival of the planning of towns as a whole, with a design and scale conducive to the human condition, has been renewed with the development of Seaside, whose construction is ordered by a plan and a zoning code. Scully observed that such codes helped create the great cities of Europe. He cited the Campos of Siena, where the law kept building facades flat to shape that great space and to protect it from projections into its public realm. We once built dignified places to live, he concluded, a supporting community, under the protection of the law. Scully assures us: we can do it again.

NOTES

i Vincent Scully, "America at the Millennium," 1999. Except where otherwise indicated, all references to quotations from Scully are drawn from his essays compiled in the publication edited by Neil Levine, *Modern Architecture and Other Essays* by Vincent Scully (Princeton: Princeton University Press, 2003). The essay titles usually are announced in the text; if not, they are cited in the notes along with page numbers.

ii Vincent Scully, "Frank Lloyd Wright and the Stuff of Dreams," p. 180.

iii Vincent Scully, *Modern Architecture: The Architecture of Democracy* (New York: George Braziller, 1961).

iv In addition to the author's personal interview with Scully, much of the biographical information in this essay is drawn from two sources: Neil Levine's "A Biographical Sketch" in *Modern Architecture and Other Essays,* and James Stevenson's "Profiles: What Seas What Shores," *New Yorker*, February 18, 1980, pp. 43 ff. Levine's introduction to the book and commentaries on the essays were also extremely useful in explaining Scully's views on architecture.

v Stevenson, "What Seas What Shores," *New Yorker*, p. 56.

vi Levine, *Modern Architecture and Other Essays,* p. 14.

vii Stevenson, "What Seas What Shores, *New Yorker*, p. 47.

viii Ibid., p. 56

ix Levine, *Modern Architecture and Other Essays*, p. 16.

x Stevenson, "What Seas What Shores," *New Yorker*, p. 57.

xi Vincent Scully, *The Earth, the Temple, and the Gods: Greek Sacred Architecture* (New Haven: Yale University Press, 1962), preface.

xii Stevenson, "What Seas What Shores," *New Yorker*, p. 57.

xiii Scully, "Architecture: The Natural and the Manmade," p. 282.

xiv Scully, "American Villas: Inventiveness in the American Suburb from Downing to Wright," p. 50.

xv Scully, "Wright vs. the International Style," p. 57.

xvi Quotations in this and the following paragraph are from Scully, "Archetype and Order in Recent American Architecture," pp. 66, 69, and 72, respectively.

xvii This and the subsequent quotations in this paragraph are from *Modern Architecture: The Architecture of Democracy,* pp. 74, 86, and 87, respectively.

xviii Vincent Scully, *American Architecture and Urbanism,* new revised edition (New York: Henry Holt and Company, 1988), p. 178.

xix This and the following quotations from "Where is Modern Architecture Going?" are found on pp. 158 and 160, respectively.

xx Scully, "The Death of the Street," p. 121.

xxi Scully, "Where is Modern Architecture Going?" p. 162.

xxii Scully, "Robert Venturi's Gentle Architecture," p. 265.

xxiii This and the following quotation are from "Everybody Needs Everything," pp. 325 and 320, respectively.

xxiv This and the following quotation are from "The Architecture of Community," p. 345 of Levine's book. In Katz's book it is found in the afterword, p. 223.

xxv Scully, *American Architecture and Urbanism,* p. 276.

xxvi Scully, "RIBA Discourse 1969: A Search for Principle between Two Wars," p. 153.

xxvii Scully, "The Architecture of Community," p. 343.

xxviii Stevenson, "What Seas What Shores," *New Yorker,* p. 64.

xxix Vincent Scully, *American Architecture and Urbanism,* p. 171.

xxx *Online News Hour,* MacNeil-Lehrer Productions, Vincent Scully interviewed by Ray Suarez, November 26, 1999.

xxxi Scully, "The Architecture of Community," p. 346.

xxxii Ibid., p. 347.

xxxiii Vincent Scully, "Urban Architecture Awakens from a Bad Dream," *Urbanities,* Autumn 1994. Downloaded from www.city-journal.org, April 7, 2004.

xxxiv Scully, "The Architecture of Community," p. 347.

xxxv Scully, "Where Is Modern Architecture Going?" p. 354.

xxxvi This was an elaboration of his views in "The Architecture of Community." Scully first gave this talk as the Jefferson Lecture sponsored by the National Endowment for the Humanities at the Kennedy Center in Washington, D.C., in 1995. The 20-minute Millennium version is noted in the first footnote on page 97.

xxxvii Ibid., p. 359.

xxxviii Ibid., p. 364.

PRIMARY REFERENCES

Levine, Neil, ed. *Modern Architecture and Other Essays* by Vincent Scully. Princeton: Princeton University Press, 2003. Vincent Scully essays cited in this chapter:

"American Villas: Inventiveness in the American Suburb from Downing to Wright" (1954)

"Archetype and Order in Recent American Architecture" (1954)

"Modern Architecture: Toward a Redefinition of Style" (1957)

"The Death of the Street" (1963)

"Doldrums in the Suburbs" (1965)

"RIBA Discourse 1969: A Search for Principle between Two Wars" (1969)

"Where is Modern Architecture Going?" (1980)

"Frank Lloyd Wright and the Stuff of Dreams" (1980)

"Robert Venturi's Gentle Architecture" (1989)

"Architecture: The Natural and the Manmade" (1991)

"Everybody Needs Everything" (1992)

"The Architecture of Community" (1994)

"America at the Millennium: Architecture and Community" (1999)

Scully, Vincent. *American Architecture and Urbanism,* new revised edition. New York: Henry Holt and Company, 1988.

Stevenson, James. "Profiles: What Seas What Shores." *New Yorker*, February 18, 1980, pp. 43 ff.

AUTHOR INTERVIEWS

Elizabeth Plater-Zyberk, dean, University of Miami Department of Architecture, May 12, 2004, by telephone.

Vincent Scully, April 13, 2004, Miami.

Robert A.M. Stern, dean, Yale School of Architecture, April 4, 2004, by telephone.

OTHER SOURCES

Scully, Vincent. "Urban Architecture Awakens from a Bad Dream." *Urbanities*, Autumn 1994. Downloaded from www.city-journal.org, April 7, 2004.

Takesuye, David. "Using the Power of Ideas to Influence Development." *Urban Land,* October 2003, pp. 140–144.

Online News Hour, MacNeil-Lehrer Productions. Vincent Scully interviewed by Ray Suarez, November 26, 1999.

Quotations from Paul Goldberger, Daniel Rose, and Elizabeth Plater-Zyberk from the award ceremony at the National Building Museum, 1999.

IF . . . WE COULD BUILD AND SUSTAIN STRONG
INNER-CITY NEIGHBORHOODS, WE'D ALL BE
WINNERS. BARON'S REMARKABLE TRACK
RECORD PROVES IT CAN BE DONE.
NEAL PEIRCE, NATIONALLY SYNDICATED
COLUMNIST

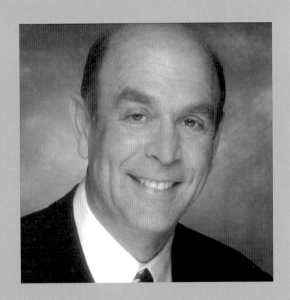

DOING WELL AT DOING GOOD

TOURISTS VISITING ST. LOUIS in the late 1950s and early 1960s flocked to Gaslight Square, an intown historic neighborhood full of bars, restaurants, antique shops, and gift stores—the kind of charmingly funky entertainment setting so popular in cities across America today. Just a decade or two later, the occasional tourist wandering into the neighborhood found drugs, prostitution, poverty, and crime; by the 1980s, the neighborhood had physically disintegrated—with buildings gone, boarded up, or on their way to falling down. Much of the residential center of St. Louis virtually vanished in the second half of the 20th century.

Huge stretches of St. Louis lie bleakly vacant where once-bustling neighborhoods were emptied of all but a few abandoned wrecks of buildings. Two-thirds of the city's population has melted away. City and business leaders have braved the tide for decades, pouring effort and funds into keeping the city's heart beating: downtown renewal, a revitalized Union Station, new stadiums, respected performance and arts centers, the refurbishment of the grand Forest Park. Nevertheless, the famous Saarinen arch, the symbolic gateway to the West, frames a downtown and inner city still struggling to be reborn.

THEY GO WHERE ANGELS FEAR TO TREAD. MAUREEN McAVEY, FORMER EXECUTIVE DIRECTOR, ST. LOUIS DEVELOPMENT CORPORATION

Yet, for a score and more of years, one man has focused on rebuilding the neighborhoods of St. Louis, on restoring the inner city as a livable community. Starting small but with a grand goal, Richard Baron is re-creating St. Louis's lost neighborhoods piece by piece, wheeling attractive mixed-income housing developments into place while restoring the social institutions so important for neighborhood livability. He has developed more than 3,300 housing units in the once-forlorn neighborhoods of St. Louis, with a thousand more under development and thousands in the planning stage. Whole neighborhoods are rising from the ground, together with reenergized schools, new community centers, assisted living centers, and even a new intown neighborhood shopping center.

Baron's efforts in St. Louis have not gone unnoticed by community leaders in other cities. Soon after his first efforts in St. Louis and nearby Kansas City, Baron's organization and talents were imported by cities across the nation—Atlanta, Minneapolis, Memphis, Los Angeles, San Francisco, Cleveland, Louisville, Pittsburgh, and New Haven, to name a few. As of 2004, Baron's firm has built projects with development costs amounting to $1.4 billion, incorporating more than 11,500 housing units and 1 million square feet of commercial space in 100 projects in 25 cities.

Baron's holistic approach to neighborhood redevelopment has proved the value and lasting vitality of mixed-income housing in inner-city locations. With each new project, Baron demonstrates the feasibility of attracting multitudes of families to reestablish the living fabric of America's urban places.

DRIVEN TO SERVE

Richard Baron was born in Detroit in 1942 during a time when that city was drawing a jumble of ethnic groups from many parts of the world. The resurgence of manufacturing during World War II brought waves of migrants to Detroit. It provided jobs for whites and blacks from the South, for Poles, Ukrainians, and other peoples uprooted by the war or fleeing the Holocaust, and for groups as disparate as French Canadians and Lebanese simply seeking a better life. Baron's grandfather had immigrated to Detroit from Russia in 1905 and established the Midwest Woolen Company to sell soft goods. Baron, who helped out in the store during school vacations, remembers the broad diversity of customers from the surrounding neighborhoods, an experience he believes prepared him for a lifelong commitment to helping inner-city families. He grew up in northwest Detroit, living with his parents and a sister in a modest, working-class neighborhood.

MY GRANDFATHER UNDERSTOOD IT WAS IMPORTANT TO SHARE, AND IN THE END IF YOU DID THE RIGHT THING EVERYTHING WOULD WORK OUT. RICHARD BARON

Fascinated by the social and economic dynamics of urban areas, Baron majored in political science at Oberlin College in Ohio. He put his newfound knowledge to work in his junior year when, during a Cleveland teachers' strike, he spent weeks as a volunteer teacher in the "freedom school" operating in the basement of a Baptist church in the impoverished Hough neighborhood.

This experience, added to his observations of the spiraling degradation of inner-city Detroit, confirmed in his mind the tragedy of central-city decay. In both Cleveland and Detroit, he saw minority families enduring massive slum clearance programs and being relocated to fearsomely large low-rent housing projects. He realized, as he said later, "the neighborhoods were going to hell and there was no one to help them."[i] His worst fears were confirmed when a weeklong riot broke out in Detroit in 1967 that resulted in 43 deaths and property damage of $45 million. A year later, riots after Martin Luther King's assassination ravaged both Detroit and Cleveland, including the Hough neighborhood where Baron had taught. (It is not difficult to imagine Baron's satisfaction in returning to Hough decades later to develop a mixed-income residential project in Lexington Village.)

Baron received his Oberlin degree in 1964, then moved west to obtain a master's degree from the University of California at Berkeley just a year later. He returned to Michigan to obtain a law degree from the University of Michigan, in 1968. Although he spent two summers in law school working in Washington, D.C., for the U.S. Office of Management and Budget, his thoughts increasingly turned to serving communities of the disaffected and forgotten minorities in inner cities.

Baron's coming-of-age, like many of his generation, was influenced by the idealism and anti-establishment attitude of the mid-1960s. He remains even today a man with a mission. His Midwestern, plainspoken ways mask an iron conviction to rebuild inner cities for the benefit of longtime inner-city populations. In appearance a mild-mannered "regular guy," Baron comes alive talking about his projects, especially the next one. He's a crusader under wraps. One of his partners, Tony Salazar, emphasizes his visionary traits:

Baron received an honorary degree from St. Louis University in recognition of his many contributions to the community.

> "Richard will come to L.A. to look at a possible project and we'll walk around and kick the dirt and look at things. Richard immediately begins to pick out the site's salient features: how the street pattern hooks into surrounding neighborhoods, special buildings that can be saved to establish a special character for a project, potential orientations of new buildings to connect to the neighbor-hood, how future residents can access community activities—all the opportunities the site offers. He immediately starts to blend all these impressions into a plan—really a vision of a great, not just a good, project."

Upon receiving his law degree, he decided to dedicate a few years of his early career to public service. A first step was to be accepted as a fellow in the University of Pennsylvania's Reginald Heber Smith program, associated with the poverty program of the U.S. Office of Economic Opportunity. The program placed fellows with Legal Aid programs committed to overcoming problems that indigents often encountered, such as job discrimination, consumer fraud, and unfair housing practices. Baron chose to work with the Legal Aid Society of St. Louis, the home of a college roommate and a location reasonably near Detroit.

When Baron arrived at the Legal Aid Society in St. Louis, the office had nine attorneys and a busy schedule. Eventually, Baron began to focus his attention on housing-related issues. What he calls a "career-changing event" came with a rent strike by residents of the St. Louis Housing Authority's projects (including the infamous Pruitt-Igoe high rises). At that time, the federal public housing program provided no money for local housing authorities to cover operating costs and had imposed no limit on rent hikes. Over the years, the St. Louis Authority had routinely raised rents to cover operating costs, to the point where many residents, especially those dependent on welfare payments, were paying half or more of their income for rent, and many were being forced to seek housing elsewhere. Representing the tenants, Baron worked closely with Harold Gibbons, the president of Local 688 of the Teamsters Union and a well-respected social reformer assigned by the mayor to mediate an agreement between residents and the housing authority. More important, in light of subsequent relationships, was the opportunity to engage in face-to-face negotiations with Gibbons's aide, Terence McCormack. Settlement of the strike led to reorganization of the housing authority, the creation of the St. Louis Civic Alliance for Housing, and the "Brooke" amendment in 1970 of the federal public housing law to impose a cap on rent based on household income, as well as an operating subsidy to local housing authorities.

McCormack House—a facility for seniors—was named after Baron's first partner who had a great interest in developing affordable housing for seniors.

Baron left the Legal Aid Society for private practice in 1971 to focus on public interest cases, civil rights, and tenants' rights. One client was the Tenant Affairs Board of St. Louis, for which he was general counsel. His growing familiarity with the management aspects of housing for low-income families was strengthened when Harold Gibbons commissioned him to evaluate an idea about tenant organizations themselves managing their public housing. "The question then, as now," says Baron, "was how to give people the power to control their environment."[ii]

ESTABLISHING THE BRAND

When Gibbons retired in 1972, Baron suggested to McCormack that they form a company to focus on projects that would serve low-income residents. They set up shop as McCormack Baron with a capitalization of $500 apiece, starting as a consulting firm, with the goal of tackling development in a few years.

By 1977, the partners were ready and chose as their first development project the renovation of the historic Washington Hotel in St. Louis under the Section 8 federal housing program to create apartments for low-income households. A second Section 8 project involved converting a building called the "Hat Factory" into housing for the elderly. Shortly after completion of these projects, they started getting calls from other communities; they developed housing projects in Jersey City, New Jersey, and Louisville, Kentucky.

But in 1981, Terence McCormack died suddenly from a pulmonary embolism. Baron was left to guide the firm's future work, and after completing the first few projects, Baron became increasingly dissatisfied with developing individual buildings. He realized that they produced little leverage to stimulate neighborhood revitalization and were too small to begin a process of change over a wide area. Viewing the bleak vistas in central St. Louis and other cities, he longed for opportunities to build whole neighborhoods that would restore the living environments of inner-city residents. "We realized," says Baron, "if we wanted to really rebuild communities, we would have to get involved with larger projects and do more in the way of building community."iii

McCormack Baron's first foray into large-scale neighborhood redevelopment, however, occurred in Kansas City. In 1982, Tony Salazar, then on the staff of the Kansas City Neighborhood Alliance, invited the firm to partner with the alliance to develop a proposed project near downtown. But another site known as Quality Hill captured Richard Baron's interest.iv Located on a bluff overlooking downtown, Quality Hill had been settled in the mid-1800s and had become one of the most fashionable addresses in Kansas City. The location of a slaughterhouse nearby doomed it to decline but years later, with the slaughterhouse gone, the area still offered elegant, if rundown, Victorian homes and hotels within a well-defined neighborhood marked by a historic golden-domed cathedral.

Baron saw an opportunity in Kansas City's rundown Quality Hill neighborhood.

Baron convinced community leaders to concentrate renewal efforts on this neighborhood. He formed a public/private partnership with the alliance to renovate and redevelop an 8.5-acre, six-block area—about one-third of the Quality Hill neighborhood. Three years of difficult negotiations ensued before cementing a development program. Many properties had to be purchased from a local entrepreneur who had assembled them for development but lacked financial resources to proceed. Some of the structures were badly dilapidated and required costly restoration; some were

acquired by the Historic Kansas City Foundation to prevent their demolition. Other properties were restored by their owners or were too expensive to acquire. Expenses were incurred to relocate more than 200 households and 40 small businesses; funds for public improvements and amenities had to be found. Construction and restoration finally began in 1985.

Today, after a series of development phases over a multiyear period, 15 historic buildings have been renovated and new development added to create 496 townhouse and garden apartment units principally for rent. The design

Attractive new homes join renovated residences in Quality Hill.

of new buildings incorporates the use of red brick, cut stone trim, and high ceilings to complement the appearance of the historic buildings. One-fifth of the units are income restricted for affordability. Several buildings inappropriate for residential reuse accommodate office and commercial uses, including the historic Progress Club, which was built in 1893 as a social club for prominent Jewish families, and which today is owned by the YMCA and used as a health club and meeting facility. The historic Virginia Hotel was renovated to be the headquarters of the United Way of Kansas City. The city spent over $2 million for streetscape improvements including street trees, period street lighting, and landscaped medians to calm traffic flow.

IT'S DIFFICULT TO IMAGINE ANY PROJECT HAVING MORE IMPACT THAN THIS ONE. IT REESTABLISHES DOWNTOWN AS A RESIDENTIAL COMMUNITY . . . ; IT HAS TRIGGERED OTHER SIGNIFICANT REDEVELOPMENT PROJECTS AND WILL CONTINUE TO DO SO IN THE FUTURE FOR YEARS TO COME.[V] STEVE NICELY, FORMER *KANSAS CITY STAR* COLUMNIST

McCormack Baron Salazar brought together the $55 million financing package from a combination of federal and state funds, a New York brokerage house, and an innovative private sector consortium. Led by the Hall Family Foundation, a consortium of foundations, banks, and businesses was formed to put up $4 million of patient equity (all of which was repaid with interest). This innovative financing package has since been replicated with other projects in Kansas City.

The success of Quality Hill has attracted other developers who recently have built more than 800 housing units in the area. And it resulted in Tony Salazar's joining the McCormack Baron firm. In 2002, Baron renamed the firm McCormack Baron Salazar, making Salazar a partner. The third partner is Kevin McCormack, the son of Terence McCormack, who has been with the firm since 1981.

PERFECTING THE DEVELOPMENT APPROACH

Quality Hill has all the hallmarks of McCormack Baron Salazar's approach to developing mixed-income residential neighborhoods in inner-city areas. That approach, which has evolved over 30 years, emphasizes creation of a mix of housing types and household incomes, high-quality community and unit design and construction, attention to upgrading schools and other social infra-structure, and hands-on management to maintain the asset value of the project. McCormack Baron Salazar adapts and renovates historic structures as well as constructs new buildings. Given the variety of market niches, financing sources, and community interactions required to generate these complex projects, the firm also expects to develop them in phases over an extended period, frequently ten or more years. And once developed, the firm moves in to manage the projects to maintain them as long-term assets.

Baron founded and has continued the compa-ny as a for-profit venture. Some housing activists find this perplexing in a field—low-income housing—all too often left to nonprofit organizations. But he has evolved an approach and an expertise that has proven workable, that delivers on its promises, and that benefits inner-city communities. The firm's specialized knowledge of arcane federal programs and complex financing vehicles continues to create successful projects. Not many for-profit devel-opers are willing to take on the headaches and risky rewards routinely confronted by McCor-mack Baron Salazar. And not many nonprofit organizations can bring the resources and experience to bear that the firm has assembled over the years.

The demolition of the Vaughn housing projects provided the site for the development of Murphy Park in St. Louis.

Baron views mixed-income housing as the starting point for restoring livable neighborhoods. His experience with low-income tenants of St. Louis's public housing developments convinced him that clustering low-income families in large buildings and groups of buildings was a recipe for dis-aster. He insists on a market-rate component in every large project, despite developers' frequent qualms about housing markets in central cities. Consultant Richard Ward comments that standard market studies for several of McCormack Baron Salazar's early projects would have shown them to "have no rational basis in the market." But Ward's surveys of targeted households found many

interested in moving into inner-city residential developments.[vi] The typical housing mix varies from 40 to 60 percent market-rate units and the remainder affordable units. Not only do market-rate units support a crucial layer of private first-mortgage financing but, more important, the cross section of families provides role models for children of low-income families. The market-rate households also help to attract and support retail, recreational, and health services, and often assist in establishing the political muscle necessary to win ongoing support for city services. Baron welcomes the fortunate coincidence, evident today in many cities nationwide, of a renewed interest in central city locations by old and young households.

Murphy Park, like other McCormack Baron Salazar projects, offers mixed-income housing.

Crawford Square in Pittsburgh adjoins downtown.

Mixing households of varying incomes is not an immediately salable notion in some neighborhoods. In the early planning stage of the Crawford Square development in Pittsburgh, for example, the mixed-income concept encountered strong suspicions that the project was aimed at either excluding low-income residents or including only low-income residents. The 18.5-acre site in the Hill District lay in one of the highest concentrations of low-income housing in the city, but its location—a five-minute walk from downtown—could attract the interest of higher-income households. McCormack Baron Salazar, serving as the developer and program manager for the project, convened biweekly meetings of the Hill Committee—representatives from the city's urban

renewal agency, the local community development corporation, and a committee of community residents, plus the city councilman for the area. After frank discussions of the developer's objectives for a mixed-income development and conversations with residents during a tour of the firm's projects in other cities, the Hill Committee endorsed the mixed-income concept, believing that Crawford Square would increase access to affordable housing for Hill residents instead of displacing them, and that middle- and higher-income households could bring advantages for the area. The project eventually created 426 housing units, of which 83 percent are rental, 55 percent are priced at market rates, and almost half are a mix of single-family detached and attached structures. Crawford Square looks as unlike an old-style "project" as possible. According to Vince Bennett, the project manager for McCormack Baron Salazar, "The development's design quality and income and racial diversity far exceeded the community's best expectations."[vii]

Baron cares so much about the concept of mixing incomes that he worked closely with Henry Cisneros, former secretary of housing and urban development, to craft the revised HOPE VI regulations that permit mixed-finance housing developments.

The quality of community and unit design and construction is an important factor in winning community assent, market support, and long-term sustainability. To attract market-rate residents, Baron wants to build communities that rival middle-class neighborhoods in appearance, function, and standards of construction. Affordable units are designed to be indistinguishable from market-rate units and integrated with them. Visiting Centennial Place in Atlanta, Cora McCorvey, executive director of the Minneapolis Housing Authority, was impressed enough by its design quality to invite Baron to develop a new intown community in Minneapolis. She especially noticed that public housing units could not be distinguished from market-rate units. And, she adds, "It's all done in a way so that 'market-rate' folks don't feel odd." Architect Ray Gindroz of Urban Design Associates described the application of this design approach in Pittsburgh's Crawford Square: "The buildings are designed as houses whether they are single-family houses, townhouses, or apartment houses. Their scale, materials, and architectural forms are related to typical Pittsburgh neighborhoods."[viii] In Baron's projects, two- and three-story buildings are the norm to establish a nonthreatening scale wholly differentiated from prisonlike high rises typified by the Pruitt-Igoe project. Gindroz says the challenge of designing mixed-income neighborhoods is "to create an environment

of stability and permanence while making it sociable as well." Developments are attractively landscaped, including street trees and lighting that make walking pleasurable. Developments also incorporate amenities, ranging from swimming pools and play areas to community rooms and shopping areas. Units are built to last and are equipped with efficient heating, cooling, and other mechanical systems.

Projects are designed to fit into their urban context, re-creating streetscapes that link the development with its surroundings and borrowing design details from nearby historic streets and

structures. As is apparent in the Quality Hill development, Baron delights in preserving and reusing historic buildings that give character—and value—to the area. Designs of new buildings adopt architectural details frequently borrowed from nearby historic structures and specific to each project. Yet security is valued: projects are nested between traffic arteries and few interior streets serve through-traffic; plantings and fencing connect buildings to provide defensive space and parking is located close to units; units and entry points of garden apartment buildings have security systems.

Westminster Place in St. Louis exemplifies the careful design approach espoused by Baron, although the first hurdle was convincing a skeptical market that this haven of prostitutes, drugs, and pawnshops was a suitable location for residence. Once the setting for the 1944 Judy Garland movie *Meet Me in St. Louis* and the boyhood home of T.S. Eliot, Westminster Place had many buildings demolished or damaged by fire, and others were slowly disappearing, plundered by scavengers.[ix] Nearby influences offered hope, however: the campus of St. Louis University to the south, a rebounding arts district to the east, and the private streets and grand historic homes of Forest Park to the west.

In 1983, the firm and the city proposed to designate 12 blocks on 90 acres for redevelopment as a residential and commercial community. Development of the first phase of 164 housing units

kicked off in 1985. The neighborhood's scary aspects gave pause to potential residents, but one visit to the site persuaded them that the price and amenities were right. The developer's instinct to rush development of a 145,000-square-foot shopping center at this stage also helped to establish a more positive environment. By the time the second phase of development began, it could include 28 high-end, market-rate units and 14 homes for sale to moderate-income households, as well as 84 subsidized units. Subsequent phases have produced for-sale houses at rising price levels to accompany additional affordable multifamily units. Beginning in the mid-1990s, construction of several office buildings, a church, a new magnet high school, and an assisted living facility for the elderly have helped to achieve a stable neighborhood. The most recent phase is attracting wide interest from market-rate households and includes the region's first "universal design" buildings, which are laid out to be accessible for a large range of residents, including disabled persons. They feature wider entrances, higher ceilings, lower doorway thresholds, and adjustable-height kitchen counters, and also include ground-floor live/work spaces with adjustable walls. The "6 North Apartments," now under construction, will contribute 82 units to the neighborhood.

Through all the phases of Westminster Place's development, design of buildings and streets has been a key concern. Baron describes the design features as he drives along one of the residential streets: "Here's a quiet suburban street, right? Except here it is in the city. Maturing trees along the sidewalks . . . handsome houses . . . the new urbanist style before the new urbanists invented it . . . there's a guy mowing his own lawn . . . kids can walk to school . . . a nice, safe place to live . . . in back of us, further west, we're continuing to build." Resident Carol Knoll offers her evaluation: "I chose Westminster for its architecture, location, suburban amenities and, most important, the eclectic neighbors."[x]

Westminster Place is again a livable St. Louis neighborhood.

As each phase of a development is completed and occupied, McCormack Baron Salazar shifts into a management mode. Baron is adamant that the key to sustainable inner-city development is management. In particular, he says, "All housing should be managed as though it is market rate." The firm screens all tenants and accepts only those who can demonstrate their willingness to be a positive part of the community. Altogether, the firm manages some 16,000 residential units in 17 states. Says Baron, "We manage virtually every site we've ever developed and I will never give that up." Essentially, he remarks, properties like these can only be maintained "if you are there, watching over it." Among the advantages, according to Baron, is that his projects retain almost 100 percent occupancy.

THE BUSINESS PLAN

Quizzed about the firm's business plan, its preferences for projects to take on, Baron spins out his list of "wants" when asked to consider new projects. An important consideration is scale; Baron is most interested in making a lasting impression in the marketplace, in developing projects that generate additional projects. His largest development to date is Atlanta's Centennial Place, the rebuilding of the nation's first public housing project. The 1,067 apartments of Techwood and Clark Howell Homes, built 68 years ago, have been replaced with 750 mixed-income units, assisted by a series of HOPE VI grants. The project was developed with the Integral Group and the Atlanta

Pleasant streetscapes make for pleasant living.

Housing Authority. Forty percent of the units are priced as market-rate housing, 40 percent for low-income renters, and 20 percent for moderate-income renters. The project design re-creates the original grid street system, orients buildings to the streets, and provides parking in centers of blocks. A variety of building styles, materials, and colors adds individuality to the homes. Community space and recreational facilities include a swimming pool and tot lots. The Centennial Place Elementary School and a new YMCA built on the former public housing site have added significantly to the quality of the new community.

Centennial Place: rebuilding a neighborhood in central Atlanta.

In July 2004, McCormack Baron Salazar announced initiation of the University Place project in Memphis, to be built on the site of the former Lamar Terrace public housing. Almost $23 million in HOPE VI grants will leverage over $50 million of other funding to develop more than 1,400 new housing units, a new park, new streets and other infrastructure improvements, a light-rail extension, and a comprehensive network of social services and job training for low- and moderate-income residents. The development will connect the site and its new residents to the adjacent medical center as well as to employment opportunities in the new biotech businesses nearby.

"Large," however, is relative, and Baron is willing to take on smaller projects that promise to leverage action in the surrounding area. Ninth Square in New Haven, Connecticut, is built on parts of four blocks in downtown and next to a retail mall. Begun in 1986 with initial funding from an urban development action grant, the project endured revisions in the financing plan as the state housing finance agency grappled with the implications of the then-new Low-Income Housing Tax Credit, environmental remediation requirements, the late-1980s real estate recession that put a hold on most development, and continuing political turmoil in city government. The $90 million first phase of 335 mixed-income apartments over first-floor retail shops, with two parking garages, was finally initiated in 1993. According to Susan Bryson, attorney for the project, it has become extremely popular, has generated street life, and has triggered other development. In the time-honored way of New Haven's government, the final two phases are still being negotiated.

McCormack Baron Salazar's Metro Hollywood Apartments, developed above a Metro Red Line rail station in Los Angeles, is another small project with a large benefit for low-income people. Developed through a partnership with Metro and the Hollywood Community Housing Corporation, the "transit village" development combines 120 units of affordable housing, 9,100 square feet of retail space, and a daycare center, all with immediate access to Metro trains and seven bus lines. Roger Snoble, the CEO of Metro, comments, "These kinds of transit villages transform the urban environment, creating a better quality of life for residents while dramatically improving their mobility."

The Ninth Square experience demonstrates why Baron has learned to look for strong community support, a "must have" for a developer new to the locale. The city must want to see the project succeed and be committed to promoting

IF THE CITY, CORPORATE, AND FOUNDATION LEADERSHIP IS COMMITTED, WHEN THERE'S A PROBLEM—AND THERE WILL BE PROBLEMS—THEY DON'T BOLT; WE SOLVE IT TOGETHER.
KEVIN McCORMACK

that goal by owning or otherwise controlling the site, remediating any environmental problems, and funding needed infrastructure such as public streets, landscaping, and site preparation. The business community must be supportive, especially if commercial development is planned. Also important is the involvement of an active public/private partnership with the contacts and financial backing to surmount obstacles. "Political leaders change," says Baron. "If the private sector stays in, the lenders stay in."[xi] Usually McCormack Baron Salazar partners with community development corporations to establish supportive relationships with community groups and public agencies, even helping with site security and publicizing completed units to prospective tenants.

Baron returned to Cleveland's Hough neighborhood in 1990 to undertake development of Lexington Village in the area devastated by riots in the 1960s. McCormack Baron Salazar formed a joint venture with Famicos Foundation, a community organization founded to assist in providing hous-

Centennial Place before McCormack Baron Salazar.

ing for low- and moderate-income residents of Hough. The joint venture built 277 garden and townhouse apartments for a range of household incomes. Today, an adjacent subdivision of 40 homes selling for $250,000 to $400,000 sits next to Lexington Village. Local foundations and the city provided $6 million in gap financing to launch the project. Today, the neighborhood has been rebuilt and two-thirds of the housing units are owner occupied. Councilwoman Fannie Lewis says, "I didn't want it to be public housing. I wanted it to look as good ten years down the road as it was the

day it went up. Richard was the only developer who was able to do what I envisioned . . . ." [xii]

The developer also casts a wide net for the financial resources necessary to undertake its often-risky projects. Multiple sources and complicated financial structures are the rule rather than the exception. The firm began with using Section 8 funds, then transitioned to federal low-income housing tax credits which, with historic rehabilitation tax credits where appropriate, provide equity funding for most projects. But the firm also taps funding from state housing finance agencies and federal programs, pension funds, local lenders seeking to comply with the Community Reinvestment Act, community-supportive corporations, and foundations. For example, the Parsons Place project, comprising 174 multifamily rental units in East St. Louis, Illinois, assembled tax credit funding from the Illinois Housing Development Authority; investments by the Southwestern Illinois Development Authority, the St. Clair County Transit Authority, and the Danforth Foundation; city of East St. Louis funding of public improvements through a tax increment district, the Enterprise Community, and Empowerment Zone; and investments in public facilities by the state of Illinois/Illinois First Program and the Economic Development Administration.

In recent years, HOPE VI funding has played an important role in funding several projects. McCormack Baron Salazar has made a specialty of rebuilding failed public housing projects that attract HOPE VI grants for mixed-income residential development. For example, the Centennial Place project in Atlanta used more than $23 million in HOPE VI funds over the four phases of development. To cover its administrative costs the firm once relied on a working line of credit, but after the recession beginning in 1989, Baron has sought predevelopment money from local block grants or federal program funds, and sometimes is advanced loans from foundations that are repaid at closing.

Assembling these resources is not easy. The federal low-income housing tax credit is complicated to use; in addition, use of federal funds from any source requires payment of Davis-Bacon wage rates. State and local funding sources are spread among many types of projects. This is where McCormack Baron Salazar's network of community organizations often opens up channels otherwise clogged with competing priorities. "It's always a hard sell," says Baron. "I think that the size of the projects is a little bit of a concern to people—the amount of money that we have to put together to make this happen is often millions of dollars."[xiii]

Corralling all the community and financial resources requires skill and tenaciousness. Baron says, "You have to be systems-oriented to create structures and expectations . . . [for a] holistic approach rather than one dominated by individual agencies working on individual issues." Developing in inner-city neighborhoods requires working with layers of multiple bureaucracies and managing to find a path through numerous environmental issues ranging from contaminated soils to asbestos and lead in old structures. The process requires dealing with affirmative action and supportive services programs for existing and new residents. Even finding architectural firms willing to design for these settings can be difficult. Changes in political environments add risk and uncertainty, particularly for the long-term projects McCormack Baron Salazar specializes in. For example, the public housing authority involved in San Francisco's Hayes Valley project ran through seven executive directors in six years.[xiv]

Richard Baron describes to the press his vision for New Haven's Ninth Square redevelopment.

Tony Salazar believes that the personnel of McCormack Baron are the heart of its success. All of the staff believe fervently in its mission and have a depth of expertise that results in getting the right things done in the right way. Longtime employees are many; turnover is low. Salazar believes that "holding staff has paid off; it's our greatest asset."

THE "COMMUNITY THING"

An important element of the firm's staff expertise is its capacity to look beyond the immediate concern for producing housing to reinvigorating a neighborhood's economic and social environment (and thus shoring up the lasting value of the finished residential product). That intention defines the "community thing" that Baron once said constitutes one of the core values of the firm. Baron, says Cora McCorvey of the Minneapolis Housing Authority, "has a deep sense of and an unusual sympathy with the needs of the poor" in the way he approaches development. Time and again, McCormack Baron Salazar has gone the extra mile in attending to resident needs for healthy families, opportunities to earn a living, and access to social services—none more compelling in inner-city neighborhoods than improving the quality of local schools. Baron himself has taken a lead role in promoting better schools in St. Louis and the firm actively encourages educational betterment in every neighborhood in which it works.

Baron's intense involvement in raising the quality of education in St. Louis's Jefferson and Adams elementary schools illustrates his concerns. When McCormack Baron Salazar began planning in 1996 for redevelopment of the Vaughn public housing project in St. Louis into a mixed-income development called the Residences at Murphy Park, the school situation was abysmal. Gang warfare and drug dealing confronted school children every day, while the school system's antidiscrimination and special education policies sent the neighborhood's children to more than 25 schools throughout the city. Baron became convinced that restoring the neighborhood required a school that brought neighborhood children and their families together in a facility that could serve as a multifaceted community center. He worked with the Board of Education to revamp the nearby Jefferson Elementary School as a neighborhood school, raising $3.5 million in contributions from 20 corporations

Baron helped raise funds to provide computer training at Jefferson Elementary School in Murphy Park.

to sponsor professional development training for teachers and administrators, mount special programs for students, and improve the school building. Southwestern Bell donated a state-of-the-art computer system and the University of Missouri at Columbia crafted a new curriculum. The nonprofit COVAM Community Development Corporation was formed to provide supportive services for the school and neighborhood. Today, 70 percent of the school children in the Murphy Park development are within walking distance of their schools.

WHAT IS SO INTERESTING ABOUT RICHARD IS THAT HE "FOLLOWS THE PROGRAM" IN TERMS OF DEVELOPMENT GOALS BUT ALSO STEPS OUTSIDE THE FENCE TO IDENTIFY OPPORTUNITIES THAT WILL MOVE WAY BEYOND WHAT'S EXPECTED. HE SUGGESTS LEVERAGE POINTS THAT WILL PLAY OUT OVER THE LONG TERM INTO MAJOR PLUSES. IN THIS SENSE, HE STEPS INTO THE SHOES OF A POLICY MAKER. RIP RAPSON, PRESIDENT, MCKNIGHT FOUNDATION, MINNEAPOLIS

The story of reviving Adams Elementary School is just as heartening. The building was closed in 1993 as part of a desegregation policy and its students were bused to schools across the city and into St. Louis County. As a community-driven plan for revitalizing the Forest Park Southeast neighborhood was taking shape, with McCormack Baron Salazar as program manager, Baron persuaded the Board of Education to renovate and reopen Adams Elementary School as a neighborhood asset. The $14 million renovation that took place over a ten-year period completely rehabilitated the school building; added a new wing for a gym, a cafeteria, a kitchen, and specialized classrooms; and provided an outdoor play area. The school reopened in 2001.

Baron took a giant step upward in his championing of St. Louis school improvements in his 1999 speech accepting the St. Louis Award by proposing some challenging ideas for rescuing city schools from educational ruin. A new compact among the school, civic, and business leaders must emerge, he said, "one that goes far beyond traditional mentoring programs, support for bond issues, teacher recognition, loaned executives, and donations of obsolete computers." He proposed increasing teacher salary levels to those in suburban districts, and other forms of compensation such as housing allowances that will attract and retain the most qualified teachers and principals. Comprehensive and sustained in-service training must be developed. Overcoming teacher shortages and funding limitations to reduce class sizes is critical. Middle schools that serve several elementary school areas should be eliminated to retain neighborhood identity. Up-to-date technology infrastructure should be integrated with curricula and in-service teacher training. Developing a system of preschool education can prepare children and families who need to overcome literacy shortfalls at home.

Baron led efforts to re-open the Adams School as a neighborhood asset in St. Louis.

Typical of his leadership style, Baron followed up on these ideas by helping to organize and cochairing the Vashon Compact, a partnership with the St. Louis public schools located in the city's West Central section where Baron is developing housing. The compact is now three years into a ten-year, multifaceted program to bring new life to the area by upgrading housing, health and human services, public safety, economic development, and education. More than 50 corporations, foundations, and community partners are supporting the initiative, which has brought highly qualified educators to local schools, established multimedia computer classrooms, provided air-conditioning, organized after-school and summer programs, and encouraged community volunteers and corporate partners to work with parents and teachers, all focused on improving academic achievement.[xv]

GOOD SCHOOLS DRIVE HOUSING MARKETS. THUS, LONG-TERM REDEVELOPMENT PLANS FOR A NEIGHBORHOOD MUST BE "SCHOOL-CENTERED" WHERE SCHOOLS ARE IN FACT MAGNETS— NOT AS A THEMATIC FOCUS BUT AS THE CRUCIAL INGREDIENT IN THE PROCESS OF NEIGHBORHOOD REVITALIZATION.
RICHARD BARON

Baron also has promised to work with school boards in other communities, including Minneapolis, Los Angeles, Cleveland, and Memphis, where the firm has been developing mixed-income projects.

As another aspect of community support, Baron also decided to incorporate affordable assisted living communities in his Westminster Place and Forest Park Southeast neighborhood developments—two of six projects the firm has developed in St Louis. Both facilities are named for Terence McCormack—who had had a strong interest in seniors' housing facilities—with two-thirds of the residents paying affordable rents.

In his "spare time," Baron also led the creation of the Center of Contemporary Arts (COCA), a community arts facility especially tailored for children, in the St. Louis suburb of University City.

The COCA arts facility for children in St. Louis.

Baron is an art enthusiast—he has purchased dozens of paintings and prints by St. Louis artists for the two assisted living facilities and the Westin Hotel he developed, and initiated the contemporary arts center to bring the arts to children throughout the St. Louis area. He rounded up a number of contributors to purchase and renovate a desanctified synagogue designed in 1946 by the famous architect Eric Mendelsohn. COCA serves 40,000 people annually, including city and county school students, provides after-school arts classes, summer art camps, an arts residency program, an art and technology program, and dance, music, and culinary arts programs, as well as a family theater series and the Anheuser-Busch Gallery. Many inner-city schools schedule visits to COCA to introduce students to the arts.

And, in his role as "Citizen of St. Louis," Baron took on the transformation of four dilapidated but stately warehouse buildings into a sleek downtown Westin Hotel. Baron's interest was piqued when the firm was asked to undertake a reuse feasibility study for the ten historic buildings known as Cupples Station. Long subject to controversy over restoring or demolishing them, the buildings originated as part of a megaproject of about 20 big brick warehouses built in the late 1800s over a rail line; the complex effectively controlled all freight going into and out of downtown. When the study's sponsor backed away from involvement in redevelopment, and other developers had turned thumbs down on a project, Baron decided to pick up the challenge, reckoning on his sense that the luxury end of the downtown hotel market simply was not being served. With the help of about $50 million in state and federal historic tax credits, the firm opened the hotel in 2001, an accomplishment said to be "akin to the fairy godmother turning a pumpkin into a fine coach with a hitch of mice to pull it."[xvi]

During the project design, the architects, Trivers and Associates, discovered another artifact that Baron is working to elevate into a community asset. Chouteau's Pond, once a lake lying alongside the Mississippi River, had degenerated into a sewage ditch about the time of St. Louis's great cholera epidemic of 1849. City leaders later drained the pond and buildings were erected on the land, but the water table remained some ten to 15 feet underground to plague future construction. Baron is engaged in selling the city on the idea of restoring the pond as a focal point for downtown life—in effect bringing a vestige of the Mississippi inland to the edge of downtown.

Baron's work in inner cities across the nation convinced him that more developers should become involved in large-scale infill development in central cities. To that end, he was instrumental in forming the Center for Urban Redevelopment Excellence (CUREx) at the University of Pennsylvania, with the backing of the John S. and James L. Knight Foundation, the university, and colleagues in the development industry. CUREx provides a fellowship program to place members of the next generation of neighborhood and city entrepreneurs in top development organizations all across the United States, where they can benefit from hands-on work experiences as well as mentoring from seasoned development professionals. In its first year, the program placed 11 recent graduates for two-year fellowships as program managers in redevelopment organizations.

McCormack Baron Salazar turned old warehouses into a sleek hotel.

Richard Baron has come a long way from the optimistic college student who watched the neighborhoods of Detroit and Cleveland burn and disintegrate. Today, he most likely qualifies as the most productive developer of center-city, mixed-income housing in the nation. Rip Rapson of the McKnight Foundation says, "No one else in the country has delivered the projects Baron has." When we look back 50 years from now, Rapson predicts, "Richard will be seen as the master on-the-ground community builder." Rather than turn away from the despair and dissolution of inner-city populations, Baron thrives on overcoming the complexities of rebuilding ravaged neighborhoods. His local partners in developing inner-city projects use terms like "infinitely patient," "tenacious and competent,"

WE INTEND TO EDUCATE A NEW GENERATION OF LEADERS IN COMMUNITY REDEVELOPMENT, AND RICHARD BARON IS OUR MODEL. [HE] IS ONE OF THE TRUE PIONEERS IN REVITALIZING INNER-CITY NEIGHBORHOODS, APPLYING THE BEST SKILLS AND TOOLS OF PRIVATE DEVELOPERS TO THE TASK OF REVERSING URBAN DECLINE. GARY A. HACK, DEAN OF THE GRADUATE SCHOOL OF FINE ARTS, UNIVERSITY OF PENNSYLVANIA

and "self-reflective" to describe his working style. They credit him with enjoying the people he works with even while projecting a solid assurance about reaching his goals.

Baron told the *St. Louis Post-Dispatch*: "You know, it's not as if we don't know how to revitalize neighborhoods. This isn't the 1950s or the 1960s, when we made a lot of mistakes and threw money into places like Pruitt-Igoe that turned into disaster areas. We have learned a lot since then. One thing we've learned is you don't take a large number of very poor people and stack them on top of each other. Now we know how to rebuild our cities, but private developers can't do it alone."[xvii] Asked whether he might take his expertise into suburban jurisdictions newly laboring under affordable housing problems, Baron ponders for a moment, then says, "I think there's plenty for us to do right here in the cities."

NOTES

i Diane R. Suchman, "Rebuilding America," *Urban Land,* April 1997, pp. 46 ff.

ii Harper Barnes, "A Suburb in the City," *St. Louis Post-Dispatch Magazine*, May 19, 1991, pp. 3 ff.

iii Larry Holyoke, "Urban Renewal Award: McCormack Baron & Associates Inc.," *St. Louis Business Journal,* September 13–19, 1999, p.8.

iv Many details of this project are described in D. Scott Middleton, "Quality Hill," *Project Reference File,* Urban Land Institute, vol. 20, no. 16, 1990.

v Sherrie Voss Matthews, "Building a Community, Not Just Housing," *Planning,* 2004.

vi Author's telephone interview with Richard Ward, Development Strategies, Inc., August 2004.

vii "Crawford Square, Pittsburgh, Pennsylvania," *Affordable Housing Design Advisor,* October 23, 2002.

viii Ibid.

ix Margaret Crane, "Bringing a St. Louis Wasteland to Life," *New York Times,* July 7, 1996, p. 20.

x Neal R. Peirce, "Transforming America's Inner Cities," *National Journal,* May 25, 1996, p. 1,165.

xi Suchman, "Rebuilding America," p. 50.

xii Matthews, "Building a Community."

xiii Ibid.

xiv Suchman, "Rebuilding America," p. 50.

xv "Benchmarks for Success," *The Vashon Compact,* 2003.

xvi Kathie Sutin, "The Westin Hotel at Cupples Station," *St. Louis Construction News and Review*, September/October 2000.

xvii Harper Barnes, "A Suburb in the City," *St. Louis Post-Dispatch Magazine,* May 19, 1991, p. 16.

PRIMARY REFERENCES

Barnes, Harper. "A Suburb in the City." *St. Louis Post-Dispatch Magazine*, May 19, 1991, pp. 3 ff.

Crane, Margaret. "Bringing a St. Louis Wasteland to Life." *New York Times*, July 7, 1996, p. 20.

Holyoke, Larry. "Urban Renewal Award: McCormack Baron & Associates Inc." *St. Louis Business Journal*, September 13–19, 1999, p. 8.

Matthews, Sherrie Voss. "Building a Community, Not Just Housing." *Planning*, 2004.

Peirce, Neal R. "Transforming America's Inner Cities." *National Journal*, May 25, 1996, p. 1,165.

Suchman, Diane R. "Rebuilding America." *Urban Land*, April 1997, pp. 46 ff.

Sutin, Kathie. "The Westin Hotel at Cupples Station." *St. Louis Construction News and Review*, September/October 2000.

AUTHOR INTERVIEWS

Richard Baron, McCormack Baron Salazar, July and August 2004, in person and by telephone.

Susan Bryson, Wiggin & Dana, New Haven, Connecticut, August 2004, by telephone.

Ray Gindroz, Urban Design Associates, Pittsburgh, Pennsylvania, August 2004, by telephone.

Cora McCorvey, Minneapolis Public Housing Authority, August 2004, by telephone.

Rip Rapson, president, McKnight Foundation, Minneapolis, Minnesota, July 2004, by telephone.

Tony Salazar, McCormack Baron Salazar, July 2004, by telephone.

JURIES 2000-2004

2000

Robert C. Larson
Jury Chairman
Chairman, Lazard Frères Real Estate Investors LLC, New York City

Robert Campbell
Architect; architecture critic, *Boston Globe,* Boston

Harvey Gantt
Partner, Gantt Huberman Architects, Charlotte, North Carolina

Alex Krieger
Professor, Department of Urban Planning and Design, Harvard University Graduate School of Design
Principal, Chan, Krieger & Associates, Inc., Cambridge, Massachusetts

Jaquelin T. Robertson
Principal, Cooper, Robertson and Partners, New York City

2001

Robert C. Larson
Jury Chairman
Chairman, Lazard Frères Real Estate Investors LLC, New York City

Harvey Gantt
Partner, Gantt Huberman Architects, Charlotte, North Carolina

Paul Goldberger
Architecture Critic, *New Yorker,* New York City

Alex Krieger
Professor, Department of Urban Planning and Design, Harvard University Graduate School of Design
Principal, Chan, Krieger & Associates, Inc., Cambridge, Massachusetts

Jaquelin T. Robertson
Principal, Cooper, Robertson and Partners, New York City

2002

Robert C. Larson
Jury Chairman
Chairman, Lazard Frères Real Estate Investors LLC, New York City

Joseph E. Brown
President and CEO, EDAW, Inc., San Francisco

Adele Chatfield-Taylor
President, American Academy in Rome, New York City

Paul Goldberger
Architecture Critic, *New Yorker,* New York City

Peter Rummell
Chairman and CEO, The St. Joe Company, Jacksonville, Florida

2003

Peter Rummell
Jury Chairman
Chairman and CEO, The St. Joe Company, Jacksonville, Florida

Joseph E. Brown
President and CEO, EDAW, Inc., San Francisco

Adele Chatfield-Taylor
President, American Academy in Rome, New York City

Paul Goldberger
Architecture Critic, *New Yorker,* New York City

James Ratner
CEO, Forest City Enterprises, Cleveland, Ohio

2004

Peter Rummell
Jury Chairman
Chairman and CEO, The St. Joe Company, Jacksonville, Florida

Joseph E. Brown
President and CEO, EDAW, Inc., San Francisco

Robert Campbell
Architect; architecture critic, *Boston Globe,* Boston

A. Eugene Kohn
Chairman and cofounder, Kohn Pedersen Fox (KPF), New York City

Ronald Ratner
Executive Vice President and Director, Forest City Enterprises, Cleveland, Ohio